Black Skin Care for the Practicing Professional

R.

Black Skin Care for the Practicing Professional

BY ANGELO P. THROWER, MD

MILADY
SALONOVATIONS
PUBLISHING

a division of Delmar Publishers, an International Thomson Publishing company I⊤P®

3 Columbia Circle, P.O. Box 12519 • Albany, New York 12212-2519

NOTICE TO THE READER

Publisher does not warrant or guarantee any of the products described herein or perform any independent analysis in connection with any of the product information contained herein. Publisher does not assume, and expressly disclaims, any obligation to obtain and include information other than that provided to it by the manufacturer.

The reader is expressly warned to consider and adopt all safety precautions that might be indicated by the activities herein and to avoid all potential hazards. By following the instructions contained herein, the reader willingly assumes all risks in connections with such instructions.

The publisher makes no representation or warranties of any kind, including but not limited to, the warranties of fitness for particular purpose or merchantability, nor are any such representations implied with respect to the material set forth herein, and the publisher takes no responsibility with respect to such material. The publisher shall not be liable for any special, consequential, or exemplary damages resulting, in whole or part, from the readers' use of, or reliance upon, this material.

Cover Design: Spiral Design Studio

Milady Staff
Acquisitions Editor: Pamela Lappies
Project Editor: NancyJean Downey
Production and Art/Design Coordinator: Suzanne Nelson

COPYRIGHT © 1999
Milady Publishing
(a division of Delmar Publishers)
an International Thomson Publishing company I(T)P®

Printed in Canada
Distributed simultaneously in the United States of America and Canada

For more information, contact:
Milady/SalonOvations Publishing
3 Columbia Circle, Box 12519
Albany, New York 12212-2519

1 2 3 4 5 6 7 8 9 10 XXX 04 03 02 01 00 99

Library of Congress Cataloging-in-Publication Data

Thrower, Angelo P.
    Black skin care for the practicing professional / by Angelo P. Thrower and Henry J. Gambino.
        p.   cm.
    Includes index.
    ISBN: 1-56253-352-5
    1. Skin—Care and hygiene.   2. Blacks—Health and hygiene.   I. Gambino, Henry J.   II. Title.
TT958.5.T48   1998   98-18626
616.5—DC21   CIP

Contents

Foreword

E*xcept possibly in the greater* metropolitan area of Miami, Florida, where his well-known skin care center is located, Angelo P. Thrower, MD, is not exactly a household name. And that's a shame, because he should be. Dr. Thrower is one of the most astute medical practitioners of skin care I've ever had the pleasure of meeting and working with. When it comes to knowledge of skin and its treatment, Dr. Thrower ranks at the top. When it comes to knowledge of black skin and its treatment, he is unsurpassed.

His knowledge and expertise are not limited to skin treatment. He has also formulated a line of skin, hair, and body care products designed specifically for men and women of color. These are some of the finest products I've ever sampled.

Now Dr. Thrower has put his vast knowledge of black skin and its care into a form that lets him share his expertise. This book is designed for anyone who is interested in learning more about the care of black skin, whether professional esthetician or a person interested in caring for his or her own skin. It contains information of interest not only to professional skin care workers but also to the general public. Anyone who is interested in good grooming will find much of value in these pages, which describe the differences between black and white skin as well as the problems specific to black skin, then go on to outline the proper techniques for caring for black skin, nails and hair. It is truly a major resource for this day and age.

Henry J. Gambino, PhD
Author of *Modern Esthetics*

Acknowledgments

A*lthough only the author's name* appears on the title page, no book is ever completely written by just one person. Every book becomes a cooperative affair in which a number of people contribute their time, effort, and talents to its success. This book is no exception.

I would like to thank all of those who helped me in writing this book and assisting me in seeing it through completion. This includes thanks to my good friend and colleague, Dr. Henry Gambino, the author of several books on skin care, who guided me through and helped me understand the pleasures and pitfalls of authorship.

Thanks also go to the people and companies who provided photographs and illustrations.

In addition, thanks are due to the following educators and professionals who patiently reviewed my manuscript and contributed many helpful suggestions: Rosaline Lowe, Brookline, MA; Mary Adams, Southfield, MI; Madeline Udod, Farmingville, NY; Cherie Buziak, Teaneck, NJ. Also to the editors, publishers, and production people at Milady Publishing Company.

And last, but by no means least, very special thanks go to my wife, Aldyth, for her patience and support while I struggled to get these words down on paper, and to my daughter, Ashley, my son, Alexander, and my mother, Doris Thomas, for their ongoing encouragement throughout this project.

Chapter 1

Introduction to Black Skin Care

This book provides the facts about black skin—its structure and its functions—that are important to know, and it dispels some of the myths about black skin. It also discusses the proper care of skin, in general, and the special needs of black skin, in particular. In addition, the book discusses the appendages of the skin, that is, hair and nails, also with a focus on the special needs of African-Americans.

For the purposes of this book, black skin is defined as that found in African-Americans with Negroid genetic endowment regardless of skin tone. White skin is defined as that found in Indo-Europeans with Caucasian genetic endowment regardless of skin tone.

Although all human beings belong to a single species, *Homo sapiens,* humans can be classified, albeit somewhat loosely, by racial characteristics. According to the U. S. Census Department, there are five categories of race—Black, White, Hispanic, Asian, and Native American. Although genetic differences result in a number of specific physical characteristics within racial groups, such as high cheekbones, hair texture and color, eye shape, and so forth, the most prominent difference is in skin coloration. Thus, black skin tends to have a brown coloration; white skin tends to have pink coloration; Asian skin tends to have yellow coloration; and Native American skin tends to have red coloration. However, the key word here is "tends." Skin coloration is a tendency, not an absolute, so that within groups, skin tones vary widely. Skin tones also tend to overlap among the groups. For example, black skin may range from light tan to almost ebony black; white skin may range from almost alabaster white to deep olive tones; Asian skin varies from light yellow to deep tan; and Native American skin has various tones of reddish brown. These differences are caused **solely** by the melanin content of the skin and not as a result of social class or intellectual capacity. Outside of skin coloration, there are no major physical differences from one racial group to another.

Structurally, there is very little difference between black skin and white skin. Of all the factors that impinge on the health and care of the skin, its color, whether jet black or snow white, is about the least important. When

Many factors affect the health of one's skin. Color is the least important.

assessing the health of a person's skin, a host of other factors are far more important. These include the person's genetic disposition, the environment in which the person lives, his or her socioeconomic status, and even his or her occupation. These factors, along with proper health care in general, have a stronger influence on healthy skin than skin color.

The similarities in structure and function between black skin and white skin notwithstanding, the fact remains that, even though one in eight Americans are of African-American background, most of the information available on skin care deals almost exclusively with white skin. The textbooks used to teach dermatologists, the materials used to teach estheticians, commercials on television, articles and advertisements in magazines, even pamphlets and brochures in dermatologists' offices almost exclusively use Caucasian models. But black skin and white skin differ enough to cause potential problems in diagnosing skin types and conditions due to skin color variations, and they differ enough in their response to some cosmetic and medical skin care treatments that information on these differences represents vital knowledge for professional skin care practitioners and, indeed, for anyone interested in properly caring for his or her skin.

All skin diseases that occur in white skin occur also in black skin, so the general approach to diagnosis and treatment is the same. Skin care practitioners should be aware, however, of secondary reactions that can occur. The generally darker skin colors of black skin can either mask or accentuate symptoms of skin care problems. Analysis of black skin can become somewhat more difficult as the skin tone gets darker, simply because the darker the skin, the harder it will be to see blemishes and imperfections on the skin's surface.

Misinformation and misconceptions about the incidence of disease and the "unusual" durability of black skin abound. Skin color is second only to cutaneous appendages in evoking unscientific comments and myths regarding racial superiority or inferiority. For example, black skin is generally considered oily because African-Americans' sebaceous glands are larger and more active, making their skin look shiny. The truth, however, is that sebaceous glands in black skin are the same size and produce the same amount of oil as those in white skin. Black skin looks oilier only because the sebum secretions are deposited on a darker background and, therefore, are more apparent.

Myths and misconceptions must be dispelled!

Black skin is more prone to profuse sweating than white skin, but this is because sweat glands in black skin are larger than those in white skin, not because they are more numerous. The incidence of larger sweat glands is most likely a genetic adaptation of black skin to let it release excess heat and sweat. This is necessary because black skin tends to absorb radiant energy from the sun and is subject to overheating. White skin, on the other hand, tends to reflect radiant energy, so larger sweat glands are not needed.

For the most part, epidermal skin is colorless translucent. It derives its characteristic coloration from the brown pigment, melanin, a kind of cellular dye that helps protect the body from excess ultraviolet (UV) radiation. When the body is exposed to sunlight, the melanin cells darken and provide a kind of sunshade. This is the phenomenon known as tanning. Both black skin and white skin darken with exposure to UV radiation. Both kinds of skin can suffer severe burning with excessive exposure. Because it is lighter, white skin tans and burns more quickly and easily, and the results are more evident. Because it is better protected from the harmful effects of the sun, black skin tends to stay younger looking longer than white skin.

The amount of melanin is the same in both black skin and white skin. Black skin appears darker because the color cells are larger, not because they are more numerous. In addition, as the color cells migrate to the upper layers of the skin, they break down more rapidly in white skin than in black skin.

Black skin is more prone to developing keloids, thick scars caused by fibrous growth resulting from healing of abrasions and cuts. Keloids can also form spontaneously. Black men are especially prone to keloid formation because of shaving irritation. Unevenness in pigmentation is also more evident in darker skin. Because of its coloration, heavy concentrations of dead cells on the surface, which reflect light, tend to give black skin an ashy appearance.

Keloids, hypertrophic scars, and normal scars are different. A normal scar heals at the site of injury but remains flat at that site. A hypertrophic scar heals at the site of injury but is elevated. A keloid is a scar that grows outside the original area of injury. It elevates itself and grows outward from the original area of injury, disease, or insult.

The differences between black skin and white skin notwithstanding, the fact remains that human skin requires care and treatment to fulfill its function. To perform this task, and to be aware of the special needs of black skin, skin care providers, whether salon professionals or men and women who want to take care of their skin through home care regimens, need information. This book was conceived to meet that need. Chapter 2 discusses the skin and its functions and shows the reader how to determine skin type, which is the first step in deciding proper skin care techniques. Chapter 3 provides information on various black skin conditions and disorders, with some insight into the proper treatment for those maladies. Chapter 4 presents techniques for caring for black skin, and Chapter 5 continues with a discussion on caring for black hair and nails. Chapter 6 covers makeup and makeup techniques for use with black skin. Chapter 7 covers the types and uses of various skin care products. This discussion is continued in Chapter 8, which talks about the use of herbs, essential oils, sea water, and products from the sea in skin care preparations. The book ends with a discussion of the importance of nutrition to skin care in particular and to overall health in general. The conditions and disorders discussed are illustrated in the 4-color insert.

Chapter 2

Black Skin Structure and Function

Human skin is a highly complex organ. Think of an office building that has ten floors, with each floor having a unique architectural design and housing a business providing a unique service. Like that building, the skin consists of a number of different layers, each with a specific design and function.

For the professional skin care provider, a complete understanding of the skin and its function is essential. The skin is the professional's basic working material. Just as the artist uses a blank canvas to create a work of art, so does the skin care provider use the skin as the medium to apply cleansers, toners, oils, masks, and other products, as well as his or her own personal touch, to create a healthy, attractive skin for the client. It is important to know what the skin is, its structure, its function, how it works, and what problems it can experience. Without this knowledge, it is impossible for the skin care provider to furnish thorough and appropriate care for clients.

It is just as important for consumers to understand the structure and function of the skin to properly care for their own skin. Healthy skin is vital to a healthy life. Attractive skin is vital to appearance and self-esteem. To keep skin healthy and attractive, consumers must have almost as good a knowledge of skin as professionals, both to be able to choose skin care products wisely and to judge the quality of skin care received from professional skin care providers.

SKIN—A DESCRIPTION

The skin is a marvelous fabric that is tough, waterproof, and durable, yet is soft, flexible, and elastic, as well. It is porous, so it lets the body breathe and excrete waste products; at the same time, it is virtually impenetrable to germs, pollution, and other harmful elements. The skin is firm enough to hold the body's shape, yet it is supple enough to let the body move.

Skin is the largest and most visible organ of the body. It is a multilayered sheet of epithelial tissue, that if stretched out flat, would form a blanket roughly 18 ft^2 in size. It is so complex that a piece of skin approximately 1 in^2 contains millions of cells, thousands of sensory receptors for pain, touch, heat, and cold, and hundreds of sweat and sebaceous glands. The skin varies in thickness from 0.1 to 4 mm, depending on the location. It is thickest on the palms and soles and thinnest on the eyelids.

The skin, the body's largest organ, is a tough, waterproof, firm, yet flexible covering whose health is vital to a healthy life.

The skin and its appendages—hair, nails, sweat and oil glands, nerve endings, some muscles, and the mucous membranes of the mouth, the vagina, and the anal canal—form the integument, or outer covering, of the human body. Some experts call the skin "the wrapping that contains the substance of life."

It is impossible to underestimate the importance of the skin to human life. Physiologically, the skin functions as a protective barrier, a temperature regulator, a metabolic organ, and a sensory organ. Chemically, it functions to produce glucose, lipids, and sweat and to maintain the acid mantle. Psychologically, it functions as an organ of touch, feeling, and communication with the environment and with other people.

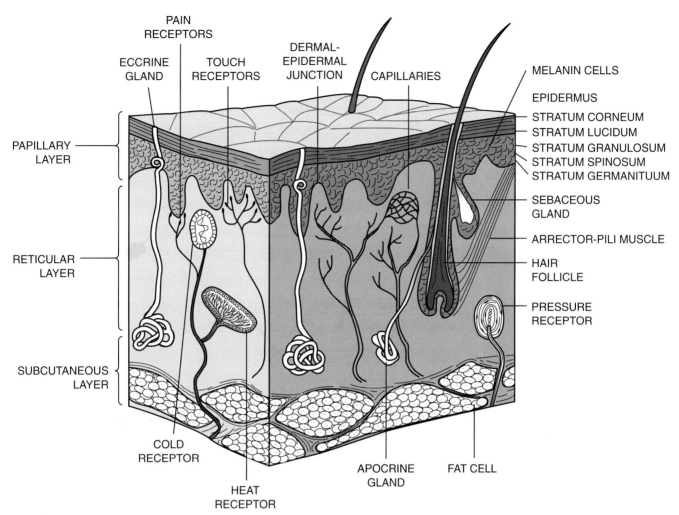

Figure 2–1
Skin structure

STRUCTURE OF THE SKIN

The skin consists of a number of separate parts that work together to perform the organ's overall function. Although the various elements are discussed separately here, it is important to remember that all of the parts interact with each other to perform their vital work in keeping the body healthy.

The skin is divided into three distinct layers—the epidermis, or outer layer; the dermis, or middle layer; and the subcutaneous, or bottom layer. Each is structurally different from the other two. The layers come together unevenly and vary in thickness depending on the location on the body and on the type of skin. In addition, a number of cutaneous appendages are embedded in or growing out of the skin. These include the hair and hair follicles, nails, sweat and oil glands, blood and lymph vessels, nerve endings, and muscles (Figure 2-1, previous page).

THE EPIDERMIS

The epidermis is the thinnest of the three layers of skin and is the layer on which the skin care provider performs all the treatments. It consists of keratinocytes, cells that make other cells, and melanocytes, cells that make color. Keratinocytes make up 95% of the tissue and melanocytes only 5%. The epidermis has five layers. From top to bottom, they are the:

The esthetician works on the epidermis—the visible outermost layer of skin.

1. *Stratum corneum,* or horny layer
2. *Stratum lucidum,* or barrier layer
3. *Stratum granulosum,* or granular layer
4. *Stratum spinosum,* or spiny or prickle cell layer
5. *Stratum germinativum,* or basal cell layer

The stratum spinosum and stratum germinativum are sometimes called collectively the *malpighian layer.*

Most of the biochemical changes that occur in the skin take place in the epidermis. Starting in the lower two layers, cells undergo mitosis and start migrating upward to the stratum corneum, where they die and slough off, performing the skin's constant process of regeneration. The epidermis contains no blood vessels or sensory receptors although a number of nerve endings are present.

Stratum Corneum

The stratum corneum, or horny layer, is the outermost layer of the epidermis. This is the part of the skin actually exposed to the environment and is the layer that gives the skin its toughness, durability, and protection. This layer is unbroken except where hair follicles or sweat pores penetrate. It is the thickest of the epidermal layers, varying from 0.6 to 0.8 mm on the soles of the feet, where it is the thickest, to less than 0.1 mm on the eyelids.

The cells in the stratum corneum are flat and have no nuclei. They are composed entirely of keratin, a nonliving substance, and are constantly being shed as they are replaced by cells moving upward from the lower layers of the epidermis. In this layer, the cornified cells have only a 7% fat content and about 10% to 25% water content remaining.

The stratum corneum has the major role in skin care. It is the layer responsible for giving the skin its texture and tone. If the layer is excessively dry, the skin will appear rough, flaky, and uneven in color. If the layer is excessively oily, the skin will appear shiny.

The stratum corneum gives skin its tone and texture and is the major focus for skin care.

Under ideal conditions, the stratum corneum exfoliates itself every 28 to 40 days, as cells migrate from the lower layers, reach the surface of the skin, die, and slough off.

Stratum Lucidum

The stratum lucidum, or barrier layer, is a thin, indistinct, poorly defined layer that varies from as little as one cell thick to a readily discernable thickness in the soles of the feet and the palms of the hand. The cells vary from a flat, dry, indistinct shape to a clear, perfectly outlined shape. They are highly keratinized and have no nuclei. This is the innermost of the two layers of dead cells.

The function of the barrier layer is not well understood, although current thought is that it acts as a barrier in some manner.

Stratum Granulosum

The stratum granulosum, or granular layer, is a transitional layer. It is the outermost of the living layers of the epidermis. As the cells continue traveling upward, they gradually undergo a transformation. They become larger and their nuclei shrink. The cells change to a polygonal shape and become coarsely granular. These granules contain a substance called *keratohyalin,* which is a precursor of *keratin.*

In the granular layer, the cells begin to die and become keratinized, starting their transformation into a hard, horny substance. At this stage, they have lost a considerable amount of fat content and moisture.

Stratum Spinosum

As the cells undergo mitosis, they are pushed upward into the stratum spinosum, or prickle cell layer, which is the upper part of the malpighian layer. This layer is several cells thick. The cells are polyhedral in shape in the lower part of the layer and progressively flatten as they rise, becoming almost tilelike. The cells are characterized by tiny fibrils that connect the cells together. These fibrils give the layer its name. Like the basal cell layer, the prickle cell layer is also a center for reproduction.

Stratum Germinativum

The stratum germinativum, or basal cell layer, is the deepest layer of the epidermis. It is in this very thin layer, only one cell deep, that the cells divide and begin their trek to the surface, a journey that will take approximately 28 days.

The cells in this layer are cube shaped or columnar and are regularly outlined. Melanin, the pigment that gives the skin its color, is also present here. The basal layer has a fat content of up to 14% and a moisture content of up to 70%.

The basal cell layer functions as the center of reproduction for the epidermis, as the cells constantly undergo mitosis.

THE DERMIS

The dermis, also called the *corium, cutis,* or *true skin,* is the thicker of the two layers and is composed mostly of fibrous materials with only a few cells of varying types. The dermis is divided into two layers, the *papillary* and the *reticular,* which are different from each other more in degree than in kind.

Papillary Layer

The papillary layer is the thinner of the dermal layers and lies just below the epidermis, forming at its surface a negative image of the bottom of the stratum germanitivum. This layer derives its name from the cone-shaped projections, or *papillae,* that extend upward into the epidermis to form the irregular peaks and valleys. The fibrous component of the papillary layer is less dense than the reticular layer and the fibers are thinner. However, it contains more cells than the reticular layer.

A network of capillaries runs through the papillae. The nutrients from the blood diffuse through the papillae to provide nourishment to the living layers of the epidermis.

The papillary layer of the dermis provides nourishment to the living layers of the epidermis.

Reticular Layer

The reticular layer is thicker and more densely packed with fibers than the papillary layer. Unlike the fiber bundles in the papillary layer, which are oriented vertically, perpendicular to the surface, the fiber bundles in the reticular layer are oriented horizontally, parallel to the surface.

Some cutaneous appendages, such as follicles and sweat and sebum glands, are found in the reticular layer, as are most of the sensory receptors and nerve endings.

Both layers, however, contain the same kinds of fibers and the same kinds of cells. The fibrous materials, *collagen, elastin,* and *reticulin,* are proteins that are formed into bundles to give the dermis its elasticity, resilience, and strength.

Collagen is the supportive component of the skin and is present in the largest amount, providing almost 75% of the fibrous bulk. It gives the skin most of its strength. Elastin is a component of the elastic fibers and gives the skin its extensibility. Reticulin is present in the smallest amount and is the least understood of the three fibrous materials. It is possible that the reticulin helps the collagen fibrils form correctly, although its exact function is not yet known.

The fibers are supported in an amorphous gel-like material called the *ground substance.* This material has no structure and is composed mostly of *mucopolysaccharides,* particularly *hyaluronic acid,* which helps retain water and hold cells together. The ground substance resists compression and acts as a shock absorber to help the skin resist pressure.

The cellular components of the dermis consist of fibroblasts, mast cells, and macrophages. *Fibroblasts* are spindle-shaped cells present in the largest amount in connective tissue. They are the cells from which the collagen and elastic fibers and ground substance are formed (Figure 2-2).

Mast cells are large oval cells that contain *histamine,* a vasodilator, and *heparin,* an anticoagulant, and are found mostly around the small blood vessels in the dermis. They help heal injury to the skin and may have some role in the regulation of lipids, the basic component of sebum (Figure 2-3).

Macrophages are large cells that are important to the immune responses of the body. They attack and degrade foreign bodies and protect against viral infections. Like the mast cells, macrophages are also involved in the production of lipids (Figure 2-4).

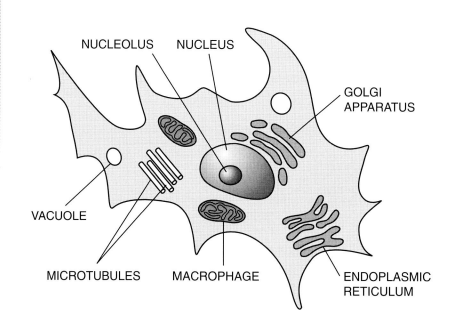

Figure 2-2
Fibroblast

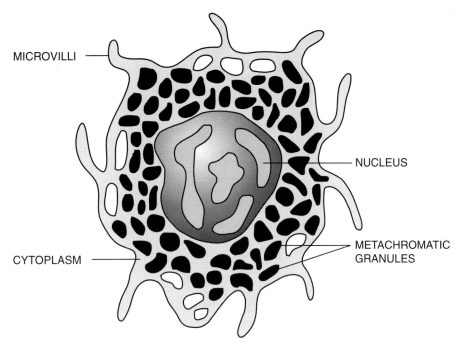

MICROVILLI

NUCLEUS

CYTOPLASM

METACHROMATIC GRANULES

Figure 2–3

Mast cell

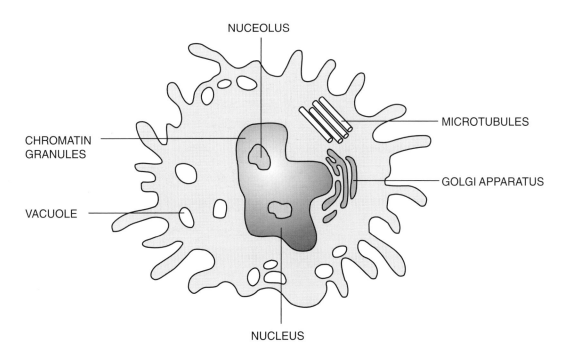

NUCEOLUS

MICROTUBULES

CHROMATIN GRANULES

GOLGI APPARATUS

VACUOLE

NUCLEUS

Figure 2–4

Macrophage

DERMAL-EPIDERMAL JUNCTION

The area in which the epidermis and dermis meet is called the *dermal-epidermal junction*. This area is highly irregular in cross section and has many cones and ridges that extend down from the epidermis into the dermis. The two layers are separated by a submicroscopic membrane, called the *basal lamina*. The function of this membrane is not fully understood, but it is probable that it has something to do with the attachment of the epidermis to the dermis.

SUBCUTANEOUS LAYER

The dermis rests on a bed of loose fatty tissue of varying thickness. This tissue is called the *subcutaneous layer* or *panniculus adiposus*. It contains a network of arteries from which capillaries branch up into the dermis. The subcutaneous layer helps cushion the skin and gives the body its shape.

CUTANEOUS APPENDAGES

The skin has a number of appendages—the hair and hair follicles, muscles, nails, sebaceous glands, sweat glands, blood vessels, lymph vessels, and nerves.

Hair and Hair Follicles

The *pilary system* consists of the hair and the hair follicles. Hair covers virtually the entire body, whether coarse and thick, as on the head or in the axillary and pubic areas, or very fine and virtually invisible, as on the rest of the body. Hair structure and function, as well as proper care of the hair, are discussed fully in Chapter 5.

The appendages are also important for overall skin health.

Muscles

The skin contains no muscle tissue except for the *arrector pili* muscles attached to each hair follicle. These small muscles are activated by the sympathetic nervous system in response to cold or emotion and cause the hair to stand erect.

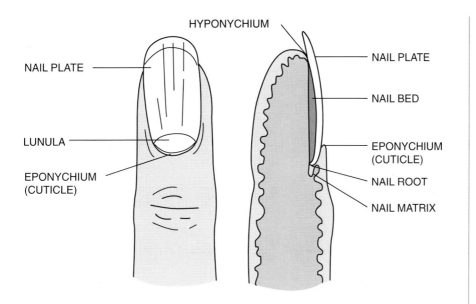

Figure 2-5
Nail structure

Nails

The *nails* are hard, highly keratinized structures located at the ends of the fingers and toes. These protective plates grow outward from the malpighian layer of the epidermis. The translucent, cornified nail plates lie on the *nail bed* formed of modified dermal tissue. The nail bed contains a large blood supply. The skin resting on the back edge of the nail plate is called the *eponychium* or *cuticle*. The crescent-shaped area just under the cuticle is called the *lunula* (Figure 2-5). Nail structure and function, as well as proper care of the nails, are fully discussed in Chapter 5.

Sebaceous Glands

The *sebaceous glands* are saclike structures attached to the hair follicles. They are found over most of the body, except for the palms and soles, and are especially prevalent on the scalp, face, back, and chest, where they number from 400 to 900 cm^2. The glands have a well-developed blood supply (Figure 2-6, next page).

The sebaceous glands produce *sebum,* an oily, waxy substance composed of various kinds of *lipids.* The sebum is secreted onto the surface of

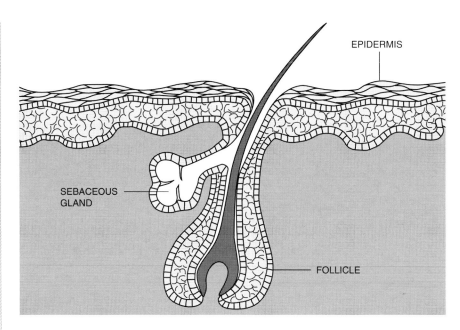

Figure 2-6
Sebaceous gland

the skin through a duct that leads directly into the follicle. Although the function of sebum is not completely understood, it is generally believed that it acts as a lubricant and emollient for the skin and has some antibacterial function as well. Some researchers feel that the prime function of sebum may be as a *pheromone,* or sex attractant, because it gives the clean body its characteristic odor.

Sweat Glands

There are two types of *sweat* or *sudoriferous* glands—*apocrine glands* and *eccrine glands.* The two types are separate and have different functions (Figures 2-7 and 2-8).

Apocrine Glands. The apocrine glands are larger than the eccrine glands and are found in the *axillae* (armpits), pubic areas, and in the outside canals of the ears. They are tightly coiled and tubular in shape. Most are contained in the dermis, although some of the larger apocrine glands extend down into the subcutaneous layer. The upper part of the coil narrows to about a third of the diameter of the lower part, then narrows even

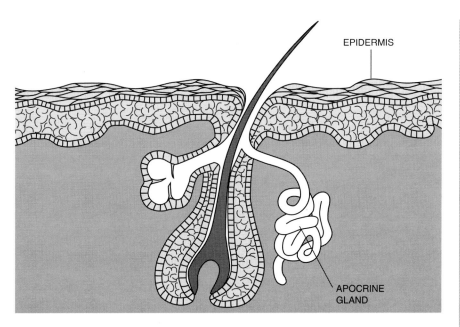

EPIDERMIS

APOCRINE
GLAND

Figure 2-7

Sweat gland (apocrine)

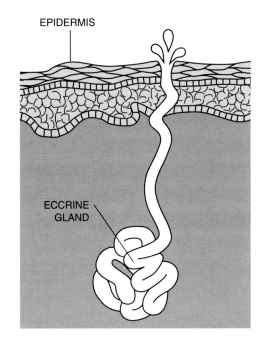

EPIDERMIS

ECCRINE
GLAND

Figure 2-8

Sweat gland (eccrine)

further into a duct that runs roughly parallel to a follicle. The duct empties into the pilary canal of the follicle at a point above the sebaceous duct.

The apocrine glands secrete small quantities of a shiny, viscous substance that can vary in color from clear to yellowish, reddish, or brownish hues. The apocrine secretion mixes with the sebum in the pilary canal. The secretion is odorless, but the decomposition of bacteria on the skin gives it its characteristic odor, especially in the armpit area.

The function of the apocrine secretion is not clear. Modern social customs governing control of body odors notwithstanding, it may be that the sweat, or more specifically its odor, is meant to be a means of chemical communication.

Eccrine Glands. The eccrine sweat glands, smaller and far more numerous than apocrine glands, total about 3 to 5 million distributed over the entire body. They are most numerous on the palms and soles and also on the head. Eccrine glands consist of a tubular secretory coil embedded in the dermis or subcutaneous layer, ending in a more narrow duct. The eccrine ducts, however, open directly onto the surface of the skin.

The eccrine glands secrete large amounts of dilute salt water. An adult man can excrete as much as 3 gallons of sweat in a day. Eccrine secretion is stimulated by heat and emotional stress. Apocrine secretion is stimulated only by emotional stress. When stimulated by heat, the forehead and neck start sweating first. The palms and soles sweat least. When stimulated by emotion, however, the palms and soles sweat profusely, as do both the eccrine and apocrine glands in the axillary area.

The eccrine glands secrete in reaction to heat and emotional stress; apocrine secretion occurs only in response to emotional stress.

The eccrine glands function as thermal regulators for the body by cooling the skin through evaporation of the perspiration. They also help regulate the salt and water balance of the body.

Blood Vessels

The skin is well supplied with blood vessels. *Arteries* and *veins* that originate in the subcutaneous layer and below, travel upward into the dermal layer where they branch into a vast network of *arterioles* and *capillaries*. The distribution of these blood vessels is complex and irregular. The dermal papillae contain capillary loops. The follicles and sudoriferous glands are intertwined with capillary networks.

The cutaneous blood vessels, like those in the rest of the body, supply oxygen and nutrients to the surrounding tissue and help carry off waste products. Because the cutaneous vessels, however, are present in much larger numbers than necessary for these strictly biologic needs of the skin, it is obvious that they have other functions as well. The major functions of the dermal blood supply are the regulation of temperature and blood pressure.

The blood vessels in the skin have a greater ability to contract and dilate than the blood vessels in the rest of the body. This ability lets them adjust the blood flow through the skin to compensate for external fluctuations in temperature and maintain a constant body temperature. They dilate and allow more blood to flow when the temperature rises to carry off excess heat; and they contract and restrict the blood flow when the temperature lowers to conserve heat. Without this ability to regulate heat, the body temperature would vary whenever the outside temperature changed.

The cutaneous blood vessels contain mechanisms called *arteriovenous anastomoses* or *shunts* that allow blood to pass directly from the arteries to veins. They act as valves, opening when the temperature rises to increase blood flow and closing when the added blood flow is not needed. This is part of the temperature regulatory system of the skin.

The other function of the shunts is to regulate blood pressure. As the vessels constrict, the pressure of the blood rises. The shunts, working almost like safety valves, open to increase the blood flow and keep the pressure in balance.

The blood supply in the skin also contributes to the skin's color, especially in Caucasians. The amount of blood and the location and density of the capillaries running below the surface of the skin play a large part in the overall coloration of the skin. For example, people with many capillaries near the surface will have a characteristically "ruddy" or reddish complexion.

Blood flow to the skin also changes in response to emotional stress, rushing to the skin, for example, with embarrassment, causing the characteristic flushing or "blush." It may also drain away from the skin, for example, with fear, causing the characteristic pallor.

Lymph Vessels

The *lymphatic system* of the skin is about as extensive as the *vascular system* and runs parallel with it. Lymphatic capillaries traverse the papillary layer of the dermis and connect with larger lymph vessels in the subcutaneous layer and eventually join the venous system near the heart. Along the way, they filter into lymph nodes.

The lymphatic system is important to maintaining the proper balance of capillary filtration. The lymph vessels remove fluids that leak from the blood vessels into the tissues, thus preventing *edema,* or swelling. They also help remove waste matter from surrounding tissues.

Nerves

As would be expected of the main sensory organ of the body, the skin contains large numbers of *afferent,* or sensory, nerve endings, especially in the fingertips. These nerve endings are of different types and register the sensations of heat and cold, touch, pressure, and pain.

Krause's end bulbs are round nerve endings that register the sensation of cold. The other thermoreceptors are *Ruffini's corpuscles* elongated, tubular nerve endings, which register the sensation of heat (Figures 2-9 and 2-10).

Meissner's corpuscles are small, oval nerve endings found in the papillary layer of the dermis. These are the tactile endings that register the sensation of light touch. The *pacinian corpuscles* are the largest nerve endings in the skin. These register the sensation of deep pressure and vibration. The sensation of pain is registered through the multitude of free nerve endings distributed throughout the skin (Figures 2-11 and 2-12, next page).

In addition to the afferent nerves, the skin also contains *efferent,* or motor, nerves under the control of the autonomic, or sympathetic, nervous

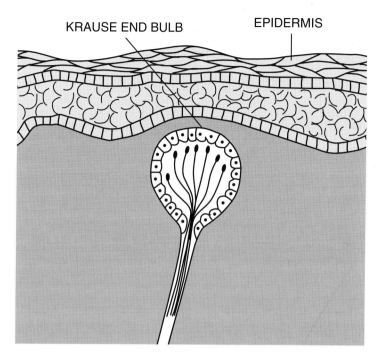

Figure 2-9

Krause end-bulb (cold receptor)

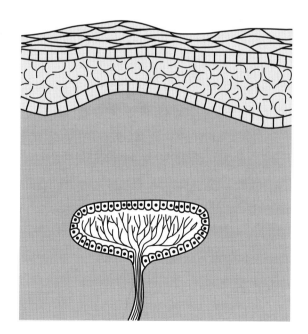

Figure 2-10

Ruffini corpuscle (heat receptor)

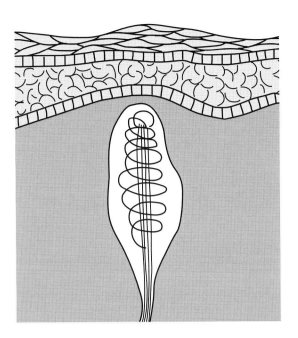

Figure 2-11
Meissner's corpuscle (touch receptor)

Figure 2-12
Pacinian corpuscle (pressure receptor)

Black Skin Care for the Practicing Professional

system. These nerves operate the arrector pili muscles, the glands, and the blood vessels.

FUNCTIONS OF THE SKIN

The skin has a number of physiologic and chemical functions. Equally important, however, is the psychological functioning of the skin. Physiologically, the skin is a protector, a regulator, and a sensory organ. Chemically, it is a producer of sebum, sweat, glucose, lipids, keratin, and melanin. Psychologically, the skin is a communicator, an arouser, and a comforter that can be a source of both pleasure and anguish. All of these functions are important—the psychological no less than the physiochemical.

Physiologic Functions of the Skin

Protection. The primary physical function of the skin is as a protective barrier. The unbroken skin keeps out harmful bacteria, dirt, and pollution. It also protects internal organs by absorbing shocks and bumps. It protects the body from the ultraviolet rays emanating from the sun.

The horny layer of the skin, that is, the outermost layer of the epidermis, is relatively impermeable to most foreign substances. The surface of the skin is covered with a thin layer of sebum. The combination of these two factors gives the skin its protective barrier function. The melanin cells in the stratum germinativum layer of the epidermis and the papillary layer of the dermis help protect the body from ultraviolet (UV) radiation by darkening on exposure and absorbing more of the sun's rays. The fat cells in the subcutaneous layer provide a cushion that absorbs the bumps and bruises of daily life, thus protecting the internal organs of the body.

The impermeability of the skin creates a protective barrier.

Temperature Regulation. The second function of the skin is as a temperature regulator for the body. It maintains the body temperature at an almost constant level of 98.6° F (37° C) through the reactions of the blood vessels and the sweat glands to heat or cold. When the body gets too hot, the blood vessels dilate to provide greater flow of blood. At the same time, the sweat glands produce sweat, which evaporates from the skin's surface to provide cooling. When the body gets too cold, the blood vessels constrict to reduce the flow of blood and conserve heat.

Sensation. The third function of the skin is as a sensory organ. Large numbers of sensory receptors for touch, pain, pressure, heat, and cold are located throughout the skin in the dermal and subcutaneous layers. These receptors respond to external stimuli and make the skin an active channel of communication—on both the physical and psychological levels. Through touching, the skin communicates much about the environment to the body—cold, heat, damp, and physical presence. It also communicates human needs, desires, affection, and personality.

Chemical Functions of the Skin

Chemically, the skin functions as a secretory organ, an excretory organ, and as a chemical factory to produce the materials needed for its own nutrition, protection, maintenance, and growth.

Secretion. The sebaceous glands secrete sebum, which is a mixture containing free fatty acids, squalene, waxes, cholesterol, and triglycerides. When the sebum reaches the surface of the skin, it mixes with the epidermal lipids, the water from the sweat glands, and the keratin of the dead cells of the stratum corneum to form an oily, viscous, slightly acid emulsion that forms a film on the surface of the skin.

Because of its oily characteristic, this film lubricates the skin and helps retain moisture to keep the skin from drying out. Its weakly acid characteristic gives it bacteriostatic and fungistatic properties. This characteristic is called the *acid mantle* of the skin and is an important concept for the esthetician to remember. The acid mantle is removed from the skin during cleansing, leaving the skin susceptible to attack by germs. Although the acid mantle will gradually reappear, it is necessary to protect the skin with a protective lotion immediately after finishing a facial.

The *pH* of the skin varies from about 3 to 9, depending on the location and the type of skin. Male skin tends to be slightly more *acidic* than female skin, which conversely, is more *alkaline*. Skin pH can be affected by environmental conditions, especially temperature.

Excretion. The skin is an important organ of excretion for the elimination of waste products from the body. Perspiration, in addition to its importance in cooling, also carries off waste materials and toxins. Sweating also helps maintain the water and salt balance of the body metabolism.

The skin is also an organ of respiration. Oxygen is absorbed through the skin. Although the amount is small compared with the amount taken in through the lungs, it is, nevertheless, important to skin metabolism. Much of the oxygen taken in through the skin is absorbed into the bloodstream. Carbon dioxide is removed from the blood and eliminated through the skin as well.

Metabolism. The chemical functions of the skin provide the energy the skin needs for its regeneration and growth. Most of the energy is supplied through respiration. A significant portion of it, however, comes from *glucose* entering the epidermis from the blood. The glucose is metabolized into *lactic acid,* which is converted to energy for growth. It is interesting to note that the amount of glucose present in the skin increases in the presence of a wound to the skin, thus hastening its recovery.

One of the most important products of skin metabolism is keratin, a sulfur-containing protein that is the major component of the epidermis, hair, and nails. There are two types of keratin—high sulfur content and low sulfur content. Epidermal keratin is of the low sulfur type, containing 2% to 4% *cystine.* Hair and nails are composed of the high sulfur type of keratin, containing up to 18% cystine. Cystine is an amino acid that contains sulfur.

The other important product of skin metabolism is *melanin,* the brown pigment that gives the skin, hair, and eyes their coloration. Melanin is necessary to human life because it protects the body from exposure to sunlight. The epidermis absorbs most of the radiation in the UV end of the spectrum. It is these rays that cause sunburn. The melanin in the skin acts as a filter by darkening on exposure. This is the phenomenon called *tanning,* which is nothing more than the protective response of the skin to exposure to UV light.

Sunlight is not all bad, however. It stimulates the production of vitamin D in the skin, and this is necessary for proper calcium metabolism.

A little sunlight is needed for healthy skin, but excessive sunlight will cause damage.

Psychological Functions of the Skin

From the psychological viewpoint, the skin can be considered the body's most important sensory organ. Tactile responses are the earliest formed and the most numerous sensory responses and are vital to the development of the person. As Ashley Montagu points out in *Touching: The Human Significance of the Skin,* "It appears probable that for human beings tactile stimulation is of fundamental significance for the development of healthy emotional or affectional relationships."

Because of its ability to receive tactile stimuli, the skin is an active channel of communication. It communicates much about the environment to the body—cold, heat, damp, physical presence, and so on. Beyond mere physical sensation, however, touching communicates much about the quality of the sensation—comfort, discomfort, affection, dislike, pleasure, or pain. Pure silk cloth, for example, which feels smooth, cool and soft, is a pleasure to hold. Steel wool, on the other hand, which feels rough and hard, is displeasing to hold. A caress is pleasant; a slap is not.

Although we do not always think of it as such, the skin is truly an organ of communication.

Affection, care, concern, anxiety, fear—almost any emotion—can be transmitted through touching. Thus, the esthetician must be alert to the psychological implications of touch when working on a client, especially during the facial massage. A lack of concern, carelessness, or roughness on the part of the esthetician will be evident to the client and will make the facial treatment less pleasurable than it should be.

SKIN TYPES

For purposes of analysis, skin can be classified according to type. The types vary according to appearance, texture, pore size, coloration, or how well or poorly the glands function. The client's skin type is the key to the treatment that will be followed and the products that will be used. Skin can be classified into six basic types—normal, oily, dry, couperose, blemished, and mature. There are variations of both characteristics and degree within each type. Note that there is no separate category for sensitive skin. All skin types may be sensitive to one degree or another at any given time. Some skin types are more sensitive than others, as well.

Normal Skin

The skin is in proper balance. The glands produce just the right amount of sebum and sweat, so the skin is properly lubricated and moistened. It has a soft, smooth texture and is clear. Pores are small to medium sized but are not evident. There are very few, if any, blemishes. Color is even and translucent. The client probably has very few problems with his or her skin, except for an occasional pimple caused by stress or minor breaking out during the menstrual cycle. Normal skin fluoresces blue-white under the Wood's lamp. This type of skin does not usually show any unusual sensitivity (Figure 2-13, next page).

Few people possess totally normal skin.

Normal skin is an ideal condition. However, very few people have normal skin.

Oily Skin

The skin is out of balance. The sebaceous glands produce more oil than is necessary for proper skin function. The skin has a rougher, thicker texture than normal skin and tends to be shiny and have a greasy feel. The pores are medium sized to enlarged and may be quite evident, especially if the skin is extremely oily. The pores will probably be clogged, and there may be a considerable number of blackheads. There may be relatively few blemishes or there may be many (Figure 2-14, next page).

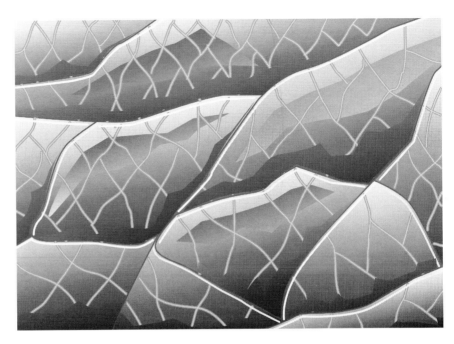

Figure 2–13

Microscopic view of normal skin around age 40

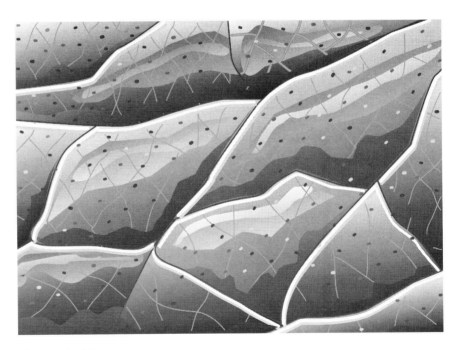

Figure 2–14

Microscopic view of oily skin

It is important to note, however, that the presence of blackheads is not necessarily a positive indication of oily skin. The blackheads could be formed by the oxidation of cosmetic products trapped inside the pores and not formed by sebum deposits. Pore size alone is not a positive indication of skin type.

Skin can be oily yet be dehydrated. This condition occurs when the pores become clogged and sebum cannot get to the surface to lubricate the skin. The skin may be erroneously classified as dry in this case. Oily skin can lack moisture, either because it has been overscrubbed or alcohol-based products have dried it out.

Skin tones can range from ruddy to sallow, depending on the amount of irritation or the amount of sebum on the skin. Oil deposits and clogged pores fluoresce orange under the Wood's lamp. Oily skin tends to be less sensitive than other types of skin, although under some circumstances, it may show considerable sensitivity.

Dry Skin

Dry skin may be oil dry, that is, the sebaceous glands do not produce enough sebum, or it may be water dry, or dehydrated, with insufficient moisture in the surface layers (Figures 2-15 and 2-16, next page). These two conditions should not be confused with oily skin that has clogged pores or that has had the oils stripped by harsh cleansing, as discussed in the section on oily skin.

Dry skin has a dull appearance without a sheen to it. Although it has a fine texture, it feels dry and rough. Pore size is small. Pores are almost invisible in extreme cases. The skin is thin. Skin is pale to white in coloration and appears almost transparent. Dead cells are usually quite evident and there may be considerable flaking. The skin may feel tight to the client. Dry skin fluoresces light to deep purple, depending on the degree of dryness. Dead cells fluoresce white. Dry skin may show some degree of sensitivity.

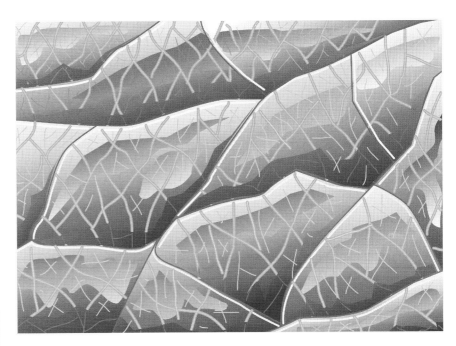

Figure 2–15

Microscopic view of dry skin with tiny wrinkles

Figure 2–16

Microscopic view of dehydrated skin

Couperose Skin

Couperose skin contains broken capillaries near the surface. These broken capillaries give the skin a "spidery" appearance. This type of skin is thin and very fragile. It will tend to be dry, also. Apart from the fine red lines, the overall color tends to be pale, although it may be quite red at times from irritation. Care must be taken when treating this type of skin. Couperose skin is usually quite sensitive.

Blemished Skin

Blemished, or acneform, skin is the most obvious of the skin types. The skin is generally extremely oily. It shows inflammation and redness and has relatively large numbers of pimples, pustules, and blackheads. Because of the inflammation, the skin is usually quite sensitive. Pores will probably be enlarged and will be clogged with excess sebum.

In many cases, the client's face will be sore because of overwashing in an attempt to clear the excess oil.

Mature Skin

Mature, or aging, skin is generally both oily and moisture dry. Character lines and wrinkles have formed. In some cases, these lines may be quite deep. The skin has lost elasticity and tends to sag, especially around the eyes, cheeks, and throat. The skin tends to be fragile and may be quite sensitive. There will probably be an abundance of dead surface cells, as well. Changes in pigmentation, such as age spots, may be present (Figure 2-17, next page).

Mature or aging skin is not confined to those of advanced years chronologically.

Aging skin may be oily instead of dry. In this case, the onset of some of the other signs of aging, such as wrinkles, will be retarded. Seborrheic keratoses may be present.

The esthetician should be alert for signs of skin cancer. If suspected carcinomas or melanomas are noted, however, the esthetician should not alarm the client but should merely suggest that he or she consult a physician.

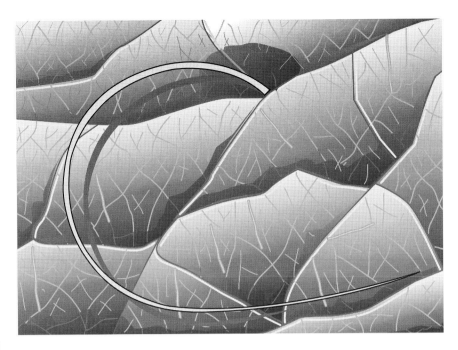

Figure 2–17
Microscopic view of aged skin

It is important to remember that aging skin is not limited to the elderly. Young people can have old skin, too, especially if they have abused it by improper care or by baking their skin in the sun.

Combination Skin

A person will rarely have skin of just one type. Most often the client will have combination skin—oily in some areas; dry in others. Blemishes may be confined to one or two small areas. The most common combination skin is oily in the "T zone," which is the forehead, nose, and chin, and dry everywhere else. As with any type of skin, the degree of oiliness or dryness varies.

Combination skin is more complicated to treat because it requires that techniques for oily skin be used on the oily areas and techniques for dry skin be used on dry areas.

Determining the skin type of the client lets the esthetician map out a strategy for the facial treatment so that the client derives its full benefit.

GENDER DIFFERENCES

Men and women are different, structurally as well as psychologically. The external physical differences are obvious. The differences that affect the skin are less so. In part, these differences stem from the predominant hormone concentration—testosterone in men, estrogen in women.

Generally, men have high testosterone levels and have larger, more dense bones and up to 20% more muscle mass. As a result, men tend to be bigger, stronger, and faster and have more endurance than women. Women, on the other hand, have high estrogen levels and tend to have more fatty tissue than men.

The distribution of fat deposits also differs between the sexes. In men, fat tends to be distributed evenly, and excessive fat tends to concentrate in the stomach area. In women, fat tends to concentrate around the breasts, hips, buttocks, and thighs. The rough, orange peel-appearing fat deposits around the thighs that some members of the beauty industry call "cellulite" occur only in women.

Hormonal differences also account for differences in hair growth and distribution between the sexes. Men have thicker, coarser, more evenly distributed hair on their bodies and faces and are more prone to genetic baldness than women.

When it comes to skin, however, the differences are slight and subtle indeed. A woman's skin tends to have smaller sebaceous glands than a man's skin. In addition, a woman's sebum production is influenced by her estrogen level. Once a woman reaches menopause and her estrogen level drops, her skin's production of sebum also diminishes. Men, on the other hand, produce sebum in larger amounts with no corresponding decrease in sebum production with age. This makes men more prone to acne than women. In addition, female skin tends to be thinner, finer, and more alkaline than male skin. Women tend to perspire less than men.

From the viewpoint of the esthetician, there are few differences in treatment for male or female skin. Analysis remains an important step. Male skin will tend toward oiliness, be more prone to acne, and be affect-

> Gender differences in skin arise partly from differences in the predominant hormone concentrations. However, differences in treatment of male and female skin are few.

ed more by environmental dirt and pollution. Men will tend to have fewer wrinkles than women and will tend to have fewer concentrations of dead cells on the skin surface, simply because daily shaving removes them constantly. However, beard stubble may interfere with some steps during a facial. Generally, estheticians will be able to use the same techniques and products they would use on female skin.

Clinical Diagnosis

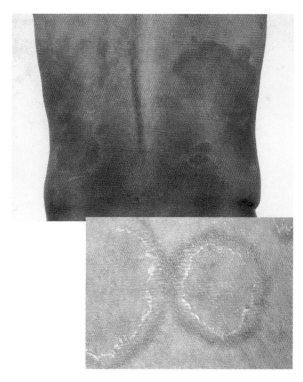

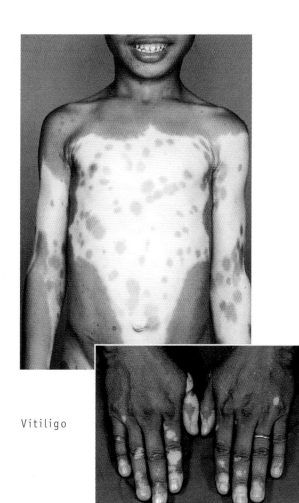

Annular Erythema — Lower picture shows a typical example in white skin. No erythema is seen in black skin, but the lesions are annular, with fine scaling and post-inflammatory hyperpigmentation.

Vitiligo

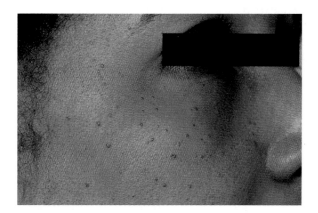

Dermatosis Papulosa Nigra — Commonly seen only in black skin and similar to a seborrhoeic keratosis, this photo depicts multiple, tiny, black warty lesions on a woman of Afro-Carribean origin.

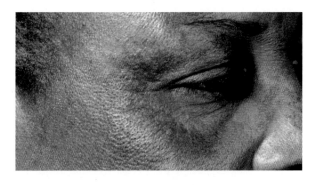

Acquired Ochronosis (on the cheek)

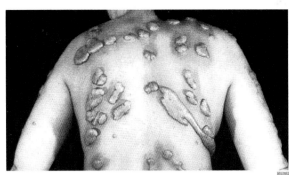

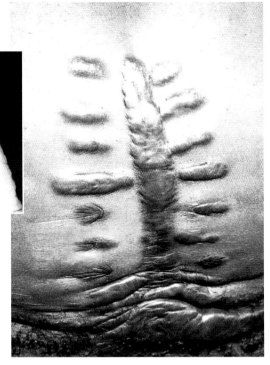

Keloids — Above photo shows hyperpigmented keloids, right photo shows keloids resulting from abdominal operation.

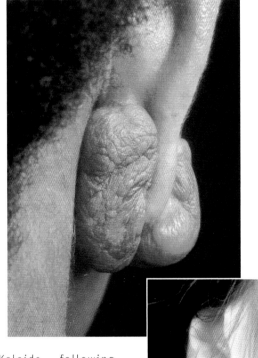

Acne Keloidalis Nuchae

Keloids— following piercing of the ear lobes.

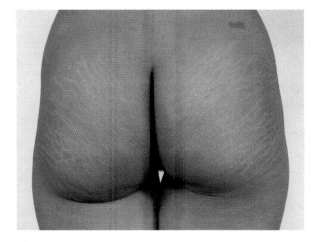

Striae — They are commonly hypopigmented in deeply pigmented skin, as opposed to white skin, when they are reddish-purple in color.

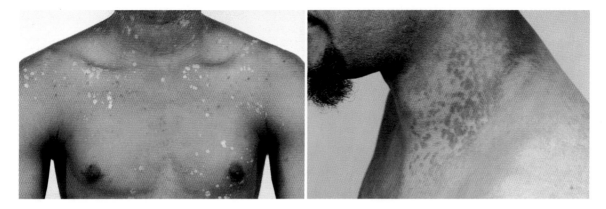

Pityriasis Versicolor — In black skin, proliferation of the yeast may lead to hypopigmentation (left photo) or hyperpigmentation (right photo).

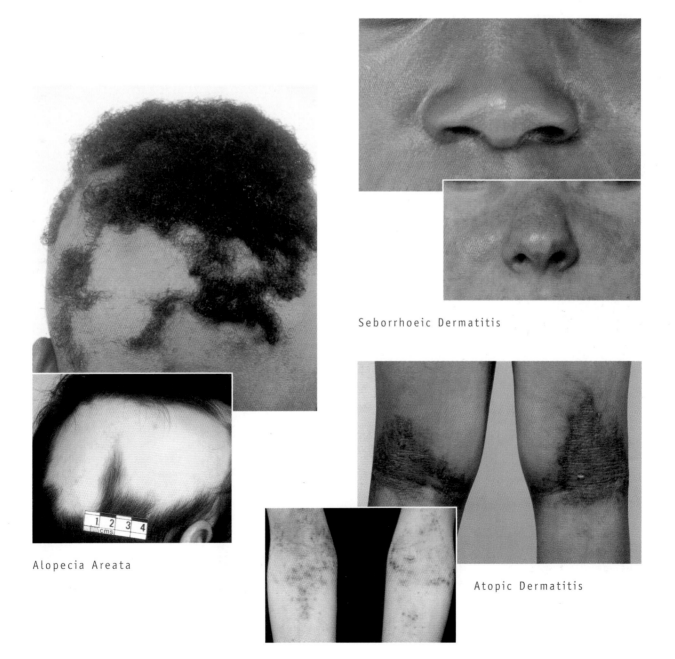

Seborrhoeic Dermatitis

Alopecia Areata

Atopic Dermatitis

Nail Varnish
Dermatitis

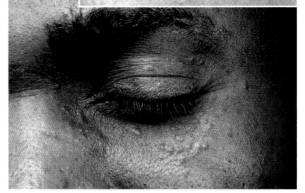

Syringomas (hidrocystadenomas)

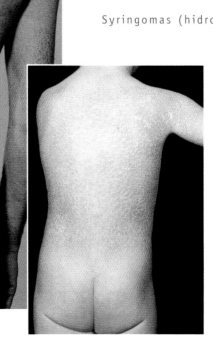

Ichthyosis — Although
a non-inflammatory
disease, black skin
may have prominent
hyperpigmentation.

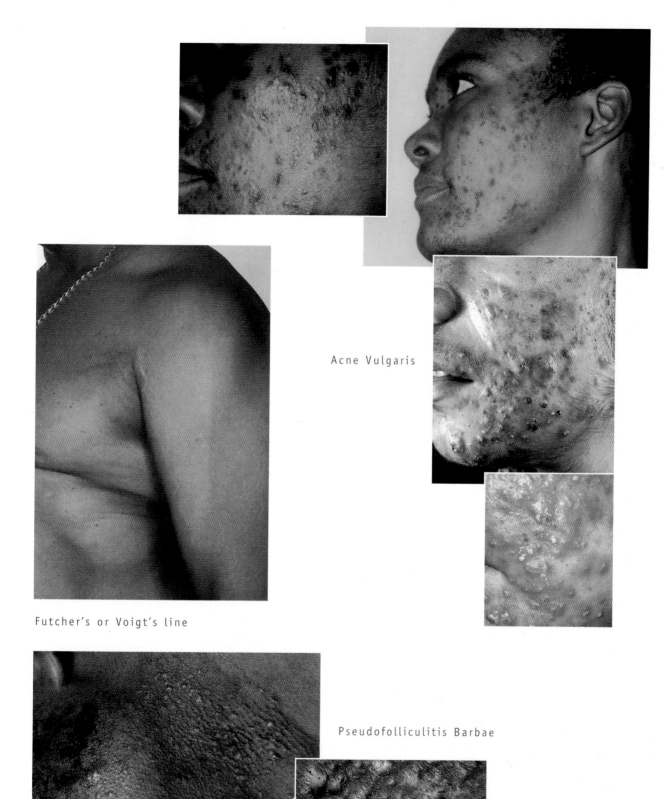

Acne Vulgaris

Futcher's or Voigt's line

Pseudofolliculitis Barbae

(close up)

Beautiful
Results

Chapter 3

Black Skin Conditions and Disorders

Perfect *skin is firm and moist,* has good elasticity, and is free of blemishes. No blackheads, pimples, or other lesions mar its surface. The pores are small and virtually unnoticeable. The pigmentation is even and no discolorations are apparent. The glands produce just the right amount of sweat and sebum.

Unfortunately, perfect skin seldom exists in real life. The glands produce either too much or too little sebum. The skin is either too dry or too oily. Pigmentation is uneven and blotchy; pores are too big or too small. Or the skin has blemishes and lesions. In many cases, the skin has been damaged by lack of care and exposure to harmful practices. In other cases, the skin is damaged by a variety of disorders.

HARMFUL PRACTICES

Many practices can affect the health of the skin; including sunlight, smoking, drugs, alcohol consumption, chemicals, and aging. By understanding how these factors can damage the skin, it can be possible to either avoid them or minimize their effect altogether. Table 3-1 summarizes these practices.

Exposure to the Sun

The ultraviolet (UV) rays generated by the sun penetrate both layers of the skin and cause damage to its structure. The UV radiation dries out the skin and destroys its elasticity, resulting in wrinkling and premature aging. These adverse reactions occur over long periods of time. Overexposure to the sun in youth, as in sunbathing, is likely to cause wrinkling and other signs of aging starting in the late thirties to early forties, much sooner than would be expected through natural aging processes alone.

As will be discussed in detail in Chapter 6, overexposure to the sun is a problem for black skin as well as white skin. Even black skin tans and burns and must be protected from the harmful effects of the sun.

Black skin is not immune to the harmful effects of the sun.

Over the short term, overexposure to the sun causes the skin to burn. Even mild cases of sunburn lead to redness, soreness, and discomfort; more severe cases result in pain and nausea. If not properly treated, sunburn can become infected. Considerable evidence also indicates that long-term exposure to the sun can lead to certain forms of skin cancer.

To avoid problems in both the present and in the future, exposure to the sun should be limited. If a person feels compelled to sunbathe, exposure between 11 AM and 4 PM, when the sun's rays are the strongest, should be avoided. In addition, a good quality sunblock should always be used. The manufacturer's instructions for proper use should be followed. A sunblock will not eliminate the risk of sunburn; it only extends the time the skin may be exposed before burning begins. Also, some people are sensitive to the ingredients in sunscreens.

TABLE 3-1

Summary of Harmful Practices

Exposure to the sun

- Ultraviolet radiation from the sun damages skin structure.

- Short-term effects
  Burning, redness, soreness, pain, nausea, infection

- Long-term effects
  Premature aging of skin, dry skin, skin cancer

- Remedy
  Limit sun exposure, avoid exposure between 11 AM and
  4 PM, use sunblocks.

Smoking

- Smoke has extremely deleterious effects on the skin and body.

- Effects on skin
  Oxygen deprivation, dry skin, wrinkling, premature aging

- Effects on body
  Emphysema, cancer, heart attack

- Remedy
  Stop smoking.

Drugs

- Illicit narcotics have severe consequences on the health of
  the skin and the body. Prescription drugs can have side effects.

- Effects of narcotics
  Oxygen deprivation, dry skin, acnelike symptoms

- Effects of prescription drugs
  Hives, rashes, pigment changes, eczema

continued on next page

- Remedy
  Do not use illicit drugs, take prescription drugs cautiously and under a physician's care.

Alcohol

- Light to moderate use is not usually harmful to the skin. Excessive use can have severe effects.

- Effects on skin
  Moisture deprivation, dry skin, broken capillaries, blotching, rosacea

- Remedy
  Limit use of alcohol.

Exposure to chemicals

- Many chemical agents, regardless of source, can have harmful effects on the skin.

- Potential problem causing chemicals.
  Laundry detergents, bleaches, drain cleaners, alcohols, plasticizers, cosmetics, bee stings, poison ivy, smog, exhaust fumes, pollutants in the air

- Effects on skin
  Dryness, rashes, itching, contact dermatitis, allergic reactions, skin eruptions, bacterial infection

- Remedy
  Keep skin clean, wear rubber gloves when handling chemicals and avoid exposure as much as possible.

Aging

- With aging, physical and chemical changes in the skin structure and function occur.

continued on next page

- Changes in skin
  Thinning tissues, diminishing collagen and elastin, hardening capillaries, decreasing blood circulation, less sensitivity, oxygen and nutrient deprivation, pigment changes, development of skin growths

- Effects on skin
  Dryness, wrinkling, loss of elasticity, development of age spots, skin cracking, lines, roughness

- Remedy
  Can only retard, not stop the effects of aging. Take proper care of skin to delay effects.

Sunscreen products are rated by an SPF (sun protection factor) number that indicates the relative degree of protection. Thus, products with an SPF rating of 2 to 4 give minimal protection from sunburn while allowing considerable tanning, whereas products with an SPF rating of 8 to 15 allow virtually no tanning but give considerably more protection. Products rated above SPF 15 provide maximum protection but also can increase sensitivity.

Smoking

Smoking is one the most self-destructive acts anyone can indulge in. Smoking causes emphysema and cancer and is a major factor in the onset of heart attack. The effect of smoking on the skin is also devastating.

Nicotine contracts the small blood vessels and capillaries. As a result, blood circulation decreases, preventing the skin from receiving oxygen and nutrients, which then dries the skin and makes it prone to wrinkling and premature aging. The smoke particles also act as magnets for airborne dust and dirt, allowing the residue to settle on the skin and clog the pores. Moreover, nicotine stains the skin or gives it a yellowish hue.

Constant exposure to the smoke causes smokers to squint their eyes in reaction to the irritation of the smoke. The long-term effect of squinting is premature wrinkling.

The remedy for this harmful behavior is simple—stop smoking.

Drugs and Alcohol

The habitual use of narcotics and other illicit drugs can also have severe effects on the skin. These substances rob the skin of oxygen and essential nutrients and can leave the skin dry or cause acnelike symptoms.

Many over-the-counter and prescription drugs can produce side effects that appear as various skin disorders such as hives, rashes, eczema-like eruptions, and pigment changes.

Light to moderate use of alcohol is not generally harmful to the skin. Heavy use, however, can deprive the skin of moisture, leading to dull, dry skin. It can also cause broken capillaries, which show as red blotches under the skin. Chronic overindulgence is also linked to the development of rosacea.

Exposure to Chemicals

Chemicals, both synthetic and those found in nature, can have harmful effects on the skin, causing conditions that vary from dryness and redness to blistering and burning. Many common household chemicals, such as laundry detergents, bleaches, and drain cleaners, can cause contact dermatitis. Alcohols can dry the skin. The plasticizers in synthetic fabrics can cause rashes and itching. Cosmetics, hair dyes, nail polish, and some skin care products can cause allergic reactions in people who are sensitive to those substances. Even natural chemicals can cause severe skin eruptions in some people. Bee stings and poison ivy are common examples.

Many chemicals in our daily environment can be toxic and deleterious to the skin.

Smog, dirt particles in the air, exhaust fumes, and sulfur compounds from industrial wastes are all potentially damaging to the skin. These sulfur-containing pollutants convert to a sulfuric acid solution on contact with the skin, the same chemical process that forms acid rain. This dehydrates the skin. Similarly, airborne dirt and impurities lodge in the pores and provide breeding grounds for harmful bacteria.

Most soaps are harshly alkaline and dry the skin. The chemical reaction also strips the skin of its protective acid mantle, leaving it open to germicidal attack. Cleansers designed for use on the face are recommended instead of most soaps designed for body use.

Aging

All of the factors discussed so far have one thing in common—their effects can be eliminated by moderation, avoidance, or change of habits. No one, however, can eliminate the effects of the natural process of aging.

Everyone ages! As the body ages, physical and chemical changes in the internal structure of the skin occur, and these changes alter both the functioning of the skin and its appearance. The tissues in the dermal and subcutaneous layers become thinner. Collagen and elastin content diminish and the amount of ground substance is reduced. As the skin loses its elasticity, lines and wrinkles begin to form.

Simultaneously, the walls of the capillaries tend to harden, causing a decrease in blood circulation. The sweat glands become less active. As the skin loses some of its ability to regulate temperature, it becomes less sensitive to changes in heat and cold. The reduced circulation also diminishes the supply of oxygen and nutrients to the skin.

No one has yet found the Fountain of Youth!!

With advancing age, the sebaceous glands secrete less sebum, which means the horny layer of the epidermis dries out and tends to crack and become rough. Changes in pigmentation also occur as the skin ages. Freckles and age spots start to appear. Growths such as skin tags, keratoses, corns, and calluses develop.

These effects of aging start to appear in an individual's forties. If the skin has been damaged by long-term exposure to the sun, however, the effects may appear much earlier and will be much worse. The epidermis thickens and becomes rough and leathery, lines and wrinkles are deeper, and keratoses develop. Some of the keratoses may become malignant.

Wrinkles, lines, cracking, dryness, poor circulation, roughness, itching—these are the legacy age leaves to the skin. Proper care can retard, but not eliminate, the effects of aging on the skin.

BLACK SKIN DISORDERS

Although all skin suffers from a number of disorders, black skin can undergo a variety of reactions to insult, injury, or disease. Black skin can obscure common signs of skin disease. Erythema, or reddening, is one of the most common signs of skin disorders, as is the salmon coloration of conditions such as tinea versicolor. Black skin, however, shows a decrease in blood vessel reactivity and this can mask or reduce reddish colorations, thus delaying diagnosis of the skin disease.

Hyperpigmentation, excessive coloration, or hypopigmentation, loss of coloration, are common reactions of black skin to certain skin conditions. In many cases, the psychological effects of these are more damaging than the physical effects. Lesions that appear red, pink, or tan in white skin can appear as gray, blue, or purple in black skin.

Some conditions are described by shape, size, or texture. For example, seborrhea in white skin is usually described as a specific area of inflamed, red, flaky, and greasy skin on the scalp, eyebrows, nose, upper lip, ears, behind the ears, and the chest. Seborrhea in black skin can involve the entire scalp, face, neck, and upper torso. These areas often show deep inflammation similar to granulomas and are usually dry and flaky instead of greasy and flaky. The color of seborrhea in black skin can vary from white to black.

Location can vary also. Tinea versicolor in white skin is almost exclusively seen on the upper torso, neck, and lower face. The same areas are also affected in black skin, as are the extremities.

Black skin also has a reaction pattern not normally found in some conditions suffered by both black and white skin. Black skin tends to exaggerate the skin's response to the disease by producing follicular excitements (hair bumps), that are dry and rough to the touch. Keratosis pilaris is a follicular exaggeration condition usually seen in black people with dry skin.

Hyperpigmentation

Hyperpigmentation, or darkening of the skin, is common in most disorders of black skin. The condition is a result of trauma or disease that causes a disruption in the line between the epidermis and dermis as melanocytes that fall into the dermis are absorbed by phagocytes. This creates a big black cell that is seen through the skin as a black spot. Dark spots can also be formed in black skin by a rise in the number of color cells produced in the epidermis at the site of a skin disorder. Postinflammatory hyperpigmentation (PIH) can result from trauma or insult to the dark cells in the stratum corneum as a secondary effect of hyperkeratosis.

Hyperpigmentation is more responsive to treatment if the pigmentation disturbance is located in the epidermis. If it is located in the dermis, the condition is more resistant to treatment. Determination of the location of the pigmentation source can be made with a Wood's lamp. Under the UV radiation emitted by the Wood's lamp, epidermal hyperpigmentation fluoresces more than dermal hyperpigmentation.

This condition can also be caused by internal diseases of the body. Addison's disease, for example, is a disease of the adrenal gland that can cause generalized hyperpigmentation on pressure points, such as vertebrae, knuckles, elbows, and knees, and body folds, such as palmar creases, and the gums. Peutz-Jegher syndrome, a disease of the small intestines, can cause hyperpigmentation of the mouth, lips, and fingers. Hemochromatosis, a disease of the liver, and diabetes caused by a blood disorder can also cause generalized hyperpigmentation. Any hyperpigmentation should be evaluated by a physician.

Treatment. Treatment of hyperpigmentation of black skin can be challenging. At present, the only known treatment is bleaching the skin, which can be inconsistent or ineffective at best. Some hyperpigmentation fades with time without any treatment. Whatever the treatment, however, it is essential that the person undergoing treatment uses a sunscreen when his or her skin is exposed to the sun.

Hydroquinone is the active ingredient in all skin bleaching agents, and is the only ingredient for removing skin discoloration that has been approved by the Food and Drug Administration (FDA). This ingredient has been combined with various other ingredients to improve its consistency and effectiveness. The FDA limits the concentration of over-the-counter hydroquinone preparations to 2%, to avoid skin irritation and the development of a paradoxical form of hyperpigmentation called exogenous ochronosis.

Treatment of hyperpigmentation with hydroquinone must be done carefully.

In the controlled environment of the doctor's office, where the person can be monitored, a physician can use a concentration as high as he or she feels will be safe and effective. As a result, prescription skin lighteners tend to have higher concentrations of hydroquinone than over-the-counter formulations.

Higher concentrations, however, are not necessarily more effective or consistent in lightening the skin. The higher the concentration of hydroquinone, though, the more potential there is for skin irritation and absorption into the bloodstream, which can lead to kidney damage. Physicians often combine hydroquinone with other prescription products such as retin-A, high-potency topical steroids, and other ingredients that help make hydroquinone more effective.

Hydroquinone treats hyperpigmentation by penetrating the skin to the lower epidermis and interfering with the transfer of an amino acid that is critical in the formation of color cells. It also acts as a cytotoxic drug, killing existing melanocytes. The effect of the drug is usually reversible when use of the product is discontinued.

The skin exfoliates from the epidermis every 28 to 40 days. New cells presumably arrive with the dark spot programmed into them, thus re-creating the previously faded dark spot. It may be necessary to continue use of the hydroquinone-containing medication to prevent dark spots from recurring.

Hypopigmentation

Hypopigmentation is the opposite of hyperpigmentation and is characterized by a lack of color, which gives the skin a white appearance. Hypopigmentation is often caused by insult, injury, or diseases that interfere with the transfer of pigment particles from melanocyte cells into the surrounding skin. This results in a partial or complete loss of pigmentation.

Hypopigmentation is not as common as hyperpigmentation but can be just as psychologically devastating. Skin conditions such as seborrheac dermatitis, tinea versicolor, pityriasis alba, and eczema are commonly seen with postinflammatory hypopigmentation. Although this condition occurs in white skin as well is in black skin, it is frequently difficult to detect in white skin.

This condition may also be a marker for more serious underlying systemic diseases such as sarcoidosis, granulomatous skin disease, systemic lupus erythematous (SLE), autoimmune conditions, and subcutaneous lymphoma, a type of skin cancer.

Idiopathic Hypomelanosis Guttate

Idiopathic Hypomelanosis Guttate (IHG) is one of the very few primary conditions that cause hypopigmentation. This disorder is characterized by white specks on the lower extremities of persons with black skin. It is probably a genetic condition because it occurs frequently in family members. Fortunately, IHG is completely benign and causes no ill effects. There is no recommended treatment for the condition.

Vitiligo

Vitiligo is a skin disorder that appears as white patches that come together to erase the coloration in both small and large areas of the skin. No other symptoms are associated with this condition, which is the result of the complete destruction of melanocytes. Although found in both white and black skin, vitiligo is much more noticeable and more of a problem in black skin. Common sites for the disorder include circular openings, such as around

Vitiligo can be psychologically devastating to its victims.

the eyes, ears, mouth, nostrils, penis, and vagina, as well as on the arms, hands, feet, scalp, and beard.

Vitiligo occurs in only 1% of the population. In about half of these people, it begins before the age of 20 and is present in 33% of members of the person's family. There is no difference in incidence by sex or race. The condition is not contagious but can be psychologically devastating.

Those who suffer from this condition are usually in good health otherwise. The condition varies with each person and it is impossible to predict either the course of the condition or the extent it will reach. It often begins suddenly and progresses rapidly, and occasionally, stops, then restarts. This cycle can continue indefinitely. The skin will rarely repigment itself spontaneously.

Sufferers must be careful with exposure to the sun because they no longer have the protection of melanin in the affected areas. Sunblocks and clothing that shield them from the direct effects of the sun are important.

Treatment. Treatment for vitiligo is disappointing and, at present, is limited to either repigmentation or depigmentation. Temporary repigmentation can be achieved with the use of opaque makeup products in the desired skin color. More permanent repigmentation is recommended only for persons with limited vitiligo in small areas of the body. Treatment begins with the use of low- to high-potency steroids to the affected area twice a day for several months. The dosage depends on the effectiveness of the treatment and the presence of side effects. This treatment is generally safe and can be very effective. Note, however, that although topical steroids can be effective in repigmenting areas where the pigmentation has been destroyed, they can have the opposite effect on pigmented areas, where their use can cause hypopigmentation.

The most commonly used repigmentation treatment combines the use of the oral medication, Psoralen, with exposure to controlled amounts of UV radiation in the A-band (UVA-A). When the drug is activated by the UVA-A light, whether the light source is natural or artificial, it causes repigmentation of the melanocytes. The success of this treatment varies from person to person, but it is recommended especially for sufferers more than 20 years of age who have had the condition for less than 5 years. Recent reports indicate encouraging progress with this treatment in alleviating the condition in children over the age of 12. All candidates for this treatment, regardless of age, must be otherwise healthy and not overly sensitive to sunlight. Pregnant women should not undergo this treatment.

Depigmentation is the treatment of last resort for vitiligo. This is the process of removing all visible pigment from the skin, leaving the skin with a uniformly white appearance in black skin and, sometimes, a light pinkish color in white skin. Many sufferers of the condition prefer having skin of one uniform color as opposed to having the spotty discoloration of vitiligo. Those who do not want a completely white look can take a prescription synthetic beta-carotene (Solatene), which will produce a more normal-looking fair skin color.

The decision to undergo the depigmentation treatment can be emotionally wrenching for someone with black skin. Because the process is irreversible, the person's entire psychosocial mentality can be altered. As a result, there are very strict medical criteria for candidates for the treatment. All candidates should seek a second opinion on the desirability of the treatment. They should consider psychiatric counseling. Strong family support is important.

The decision to undergo depigmentation may be extremely difficult for a person with black skin. Psychiatric counseling and family support are important aspects.

Typical candidates for the treatment include those who failed to respond to other treatments and who are afflicted with the condition in 40% or more of their skin area.

Depigmentation is accomplished by chemically destroying all melanocytes in the skin. The hair is rarely affected and eye color is never affected by the treatment. Strict adherence to the physician's instructions during and after treatment is essential.

The chemical used is monobenzone 20% (Benoquin 20%) in the form of a cream. It is applied twice daily for 6 to 9 months for complete depigmentation of the entire body to occur. The skin must be protected from exposure to the sun while the treatment is in progress. Also, depigmentation may occur in areas where the cream has not been applied. Monobenzone should not be used on hyperpigmented lesions because the skin can develop a permanent confetti-type pigmentation.

Excessive Skin Dryness

Black skin that is excessively dry often has a gray ashy appearance. Eczema can also result from excessive dryness. This condition can be shameful to some people because others sometimes associate an ashy appearance with poor personal hygiene. Clinically, however, the ashy appearance of dry skin is caused by the reflection of light on the dead skin cells on the surface of the skin and the air beneath the scales.

Dry skin can occur anywhere on the body but is especially distressing when it occurs on the hands and feet. These are socially high-profile areas and, when dry, can be unattractive. The condition in these areas can be alleviated by regular manicures and pedicures for both men and women. Frequent use of moisturizers will help prevent dryness on the rest of the body.

Seborrheac Dermatitis

Seborrheac dermatitis is an inflammatory form of dandruff occurring on areas of the scalp, eyebrows, around the nose, the upper lip, sideburns, inside the ears, and behind the ears. It is common in black skin and often appears as a difficult case of dandruff that seems to be spreading to the face. The skin appears dry, flaky, gray, and occasionally inflamed. Hyperpigmentation and hypopigmentation are also commonly encountered with this condition.

Treatment. A predisposition to this condition makes it very difficult for black women to receive a currently fashionable treatment in the salon—hair relaxation. The chemicals used to straighten curly hair irritate the scalp. Someone suffering from seborrhea will have a chronic irritation of the scalp and, by applying the product to the scalp, receive an intense burn, which is painful and potentially damaging to the scalp, leading to scarring and hair loss. Anyone who has a scalp condition should consult with a physician familiar with black hair grooming habits before getting a treatment in a salon.

Black hair and scalp are commonly dry because of the curved nature of the hair follicle and the terminal hair. The natural oils produced in the sebaceous glands can be somewhat inconsistent in moisturizing the scalp and hair. As a result, hair oils are routinely added to black hair.

Medicated dandruff shampoos are often recommended for use by blacks suffering from seborrhea and other dry scalp problems. At times, these may not be appropriate for given hair types, styles, or conditions. Some black hair styles require high levels of moisture. If this moisture is lacking, even to a small degree, there may be severe hair breakage. Dandruff shampoos tend to be drying to the hair and scalp, and this may perpetuate the dryness innate to blacks, making the problems even worse. If dandruff shampoos are used, an oil-based conditioner should be used afterward.

Daily shampooing can exacerbate the problem of dryness in black hair.

Someone with a dry scalp often has an overwhelming temptation to wash his or her hair every day to remove the dry flakes. However, daily shampooing can exacerbate the dryness problem in black hair. Typically, black hair is shampooed once every 1 to 2 weeks, depending on the person's preferences, hair style, and oil requirement of the hair. If the oil requirement is high, the frequency of shampooing can be reduced.

Tinea Versicolor (Acid)

Tinea versicolor is a superficial fungus infection of the skin. It is not associated with any internal diseases, nor is it caused by improper diet, especially from drinking large amounts of soda. In black skin, this condition can be either hyperpigmented or hypopigmented. It is commonly found on the lower face, the upper neck, chest, and back. It is also often seen on the upper extremities.

The fungus that causes the infection is common and resides on the skin without causing the infection in most people. It does affect a small portion of the population, however. The condition is common in warm weather environments and during warm seasons when the heat and humidity conditions on which the fungus thrives are present.

The condition is not contagious and responds well to appropriate treatment. Once treatment begins, exposure to sunlight often helps repigment the skin in hypopigmented tinea versicolor.

Keloids

Keloids are a type of scar that heal differently from normal scars. *Normal scars* heal at the site of injury and are not execrated or elevated. *Hypertrophic scars* heal at the site of injury but are elevated above that site. They are firm to the touch and often are accompanied by pigmentation changes. These scars often regress spontaneously to normal scars. *Keloids* are hard, raised, hairless, shiny, smooth, large scars with clawlike protuberances that are larger than the size of the injury. They become exaggerated and extend both laterally and vertically from the site of the injury. Keloids can be very uncomfortable, unsightly, itchy, and painful, and they can become infected.

Three myths about keloid scars still are perpetuated.

Keloid scars are more common in black skin, but can be present in white skin as well. There are many myths about keloids, such as all black-skinned people are at risk for their formation; once a person has formed keloids, he or she will always form them; and cosmetic surgery will always lead to keloid scars. As a result of this last myth, many black women fear undergoing cosmetic surgery.

Causes. These unsightly lesions are usually the result of insult, injury, or chronic inflammation of the skin, especially when the skin has been broken. Insult and injury usually involve penetration of the epidermis and the papillary layer of the dermis. Chronic itching and infection prolong the infection and the healing time, stimulating additional collagen formation. *Collagen* is a protein responsible for the formation of normal scars as the substance forms and breaks down. Keloids form when this mechanism fails. In these cases, collagen is produced at a higher rate and does not break down. The scar tissue that then accumulates creates a scar that grows into the surrounding skin.

Growth factors and hormonal changes are often suggested as probable causes because keloids tend to be more common in children and young adults. They are also common during pregnancy. Family history also has a strong influence in the predilection to keloid formation.

Keloids can appear on most parts of the body except the eyelids, palms of the hands, and soles of the feet. Keloids on the ear lobes are common and result from infection and chronic irritation from having the ears pierced. They are most prevalent on the backs of the ear lobes, especially when inexpensive earring backs are used. Keloids on the hands, arms, and legs most often result from trauma, whereas those on the face, chest, and back most often result from infection. It is common for keloids to form on the abdomen and in the pelvic area after surgery. Keloids have been known to form spontaneously without any detectable cause, usually seen on the chest.

Treatment. The same basic treatments have been used for decades and are still inconsistent and ineffective. Treatment of keloids can be either medical or surgical, or a combination of both. Medical treatments include the use of topical steroids, intralesional steroids, intralesional calcium channel blockers, and hydrogel sheeting. Topical and intralesional steroids work by reducing irritation, itching, and pain. They also retard the synthesis of collagen.

Calcium channel blockers in pill form are a common medication for high blood pressure. These medicines have recently been tested for the treatment of keloids intralesionally where they seem to inhibit calcium from entering cells and helping them grow. Although definite results are not available as yet, initial impressions are encouraging.

Hydrogel sheeting offers treatment by occluding the scar. This causes compression and increases the temperature of the scar, which helps break down the collagen.

Surgical treatment involves the excision and removal of the keloid. This procedure does get rid of the keloid, but there is a risk that the keloids will return and be even bigger. The rate of recurrence can be reduced by combining medical and surgical treatments.

Pseudofolliculitis Barber

Pseudofolliculitis barber (PFB), also known as razor bump, is an inflammatory condition in which hard coarse shaved hair regrows into the skin, mimicking thousands of splinters sticking into the beard area. It occurs in areas that are shaved with a razor blade and is characterized by small and large bumps in these shaved areas. The condition leads to irritation, infection, bump formation, and discoloration of the skin.

Proper shaving technique can prevent pseudofolliculitis barber.

Although any ethnic group with coarse curly hair can be affected to some degree, PFB is primarily an affliction of African-American men. More than 12 million black men suffer from this common condition.

Women can also suffer from PFB. In women, the condition affects the skin in the bikini area, underarms, legs, and other areas that are shaved.

To some extent, PFB may be an inherited condition. But the most significant cause of the condition is improper shaving technique. For most people, knowing how to shave properly and following the correct support system will help control these unsightly shaving bumps and discolorations of the skin.

Shaving Techniques for Controlling PFB. Wash the face with a cleanser formulated for the skin type. Use the correct skin scrub as directed on the label. Rinse the face thoroughly, leaving the bearded areas wet.

Determine the direction of hair growth. For most men, beard hair growth is downward. This can be confirmed by running the fingers downward on the beard. It should feel smooth, not rough.

Apply shave cream or gel to the wet beard. Always begin the shaving process with the upper face (sideburns to upper jaw line). Start at the upper jaw line and shave to the lower jaw line using short light strokes. Finish the shaving process from the lower jaw line down to the end of the beard area. Each stroke should be feather light.

After shaving, rinse the face thoroughly. Follow any recommended treatment programs in the beard area. Pat the skin dry and use the recommended toner and treatment products.

There are a number of simple shaving tips to remember:

- Shave daily. The longer the beard grows, the more potential there is for the formation of shaving bumps.

- Shave with the sharpest blade available.

- Never shave against the direction of hair growth.

- Never pull or stretch the skin when shaving.

- Never shave repetitively over the same area. Three strokes in the same area is the limit before severe irritation occurs.

- Never shave a dirty face. Always wash the face before each shave.

- Never try to shave too close, especially in the neck area.

Acne Keloidalis

Acne keloidalis (AK) is a chronic irritation common on the scalp and lower neck of black men. It is the result of prolonged, grinding friction and irritation. AK causes dryness, itching, pain, bleeding, scarring, and keloids, as well as loss of scalp hair and infections that drain. The condition can be devastating socially. AK has reached almost epidemic proportions, rivaling PFB in black men as the greatest skin care concern.

Acne keloidalis has become a great concern of black men.

The primary cause of this condition is getting a short haircut in the lower back of the neck. For the barber to remove all the hair in this area, a substantial amount of friction and irritation is created. This causes a chronic itch, which leads to scratching, which results in even more trauma and irritation to the area. The infection takes the form of little acne bumps (folliculitis), which have the potential to develop into keloid scars.

Any kind of friction and irritation of the scalp can cause AK, for example, shaving the scalp closely with a razor, clippers, or depilatories; continued brushing and combing of the hair; using hair relaxers and hair colorants; or even wearing tight-fitting hats or helmets.

Treatment consists of avoiding the services or products that cause chronic scalp irritation. Medical treatments are based on the form of the condition at the time treatment is started. Infections are usually treated with oral antibiotics and maximum strength acne medications. Scars are treated the same as keloids. Nodules, cysts, and sinus tract infections are treated with isotretinoin (Accutane).

Dermatosis Papulosa Nigra

Dermatosis papulosa nigra (DPN) is a condition involving hereditary lesions that first appear as black pin dots and develop into wartlike growths on the skin, which increase in size and numbers over a period of years. Growth rate and size usually slow down during the fifth or sixth decade. Lesion size ranges from 1 to 8 mm in diameter and can be elevated from 1 to 3 mm above the skin. Older lesions can become very long and peduculated or filiform.

These lesions begin to appear in adolescence or early adulthood. They are common on the face and neck, especially on the upper cheek area. They can, however, form on almost any area of the body. Any one individual can have hundreds, even thousands, of these lesions.

This condition is more common in women than in men, but is almost exclusively limited to black skin and affects up to 35% of the black population of the United States. DPN lesions are benign epidermal tumors and are not known to become malignant. They are usually free of pain and itching, although these can develop if the lesions become large and are irritated by friction from clothing. The lesions may hang over the eyelids and obstruct vision. Many sufferers of this condition, however, are more concerned with the cosmetic effects of the lesions than with health effects, and these concerns are usually the spur to seek treatment.

Treatment is usually surgical. Electrodessication and curettage (ED&C) is a common and accepted technique for removing DPN lesions. The results are normally successful when the procedure is done by an experienced practitioner and follow-up care is given. Some degree of hypopigmentation or hyperpigmentation can be expected. Cryotherapy is also used but should be undertaken with caution because of the potential for hypopigmentation in black skin.

CANCER IN BLACK SKIN

The prevalence of skin cancer is one of the indications that black skin and white skin respond differently to insult and injury. Both black-skinned people and white-skinned people suffer from skin cancers. The most common cause of cancer in white skin is overexposure to UV radiation from the sun. The most common causes of cancer in black skin, however, are trauma and chronic disease.

Whites tend to fear UV radiation because of health issues. Blacks' concern with UV radiation stems from cosmetic issues. With black skin, the major cosmetic complaint is skin discoloration. UV light turns black skin darker by stimulating melanin production and darkening the skin, either evenly or in spots. Black-skinned consumers tend to wear skin protection to minimize skin discoloration; white-skinned consumers wear skin protection as a shield against cancer. This makes perfect sense because the prevalence of cancer in white skin from sun exposure is disproportionately high. Black skin is protected by the larger, more evenly dispersed melanocyte granules in the epidermis.

Although millions of dollars are spent annually for identifying risk factors, counseling, early detection, and the formulation of products for prevention of skin cancer in white skin, very little is spent on research into the risk factors leading to cancer in black skin. These factors should receive similar medical attention and appropriate financial support.

Treatment for all skin cancers is the same for both black skin and white skin. Drugs, surgery, and chemotherapy are used in treatment regimens.

Squamous Cell Carcinoma

Squamous cell carcinoma is more common in white skin but it is the most common form of skin cancer among blacks. In whites, this form of cancer

Blacks and whites fear the sun's ultraviolet rays—but for different reasons.

is most often associated with sun exposure. Carcinomas most frequently appear in those areas of the body most open to the sun, such as the face, head, and neck. In blacks, these carcinomas are found at the site of traumatic injury or chronic disease and appear frequently on the lower extremities. The mortality rate for squamous cell cancer is higher for those with black skin than for people with white skin. This is most likely a result of later detection because of the lack of information on risk factors distributed to health care providers and to the general public.

Basal Cell Carcinoma

Basal cell carcinoma is the most common skin cancer among whites and, like squamous cell cancer, is caused by prolonged sun exposure. This form of skin cancer is found just as frequently on sun exposed areas in black skin.

Melanoma

Melanoma is the most life-threatening form of skin cancer and is more common on white skin than black skin. Melanomas on white skin are most often found on areas exposed to the sun; on black skin, they are found most often on the palms of the hands and the soles of the feet.

Melanomas are very difficult to diagnose on black skin. In addition, black skin melanomas are inclined to metastasize more aggressively, probably because detection tends to be later and the melanomas are located in areas where the course of the disease is naturally more aggressive.

ACNE

Acne is one of the most common skin disorders and, at any one time, is shared by at least 20 million people in varying degrees of severity. The disorder affects all ethnic groups. Blacks and whites both suffer extensively from acne. However, the aftereffects of acne in black skin can be painfully disfiguring and long lasting, leaving scars and discoloration that can impair self-esteem.

Acne is prevalent in 85% of people aged from 12 to 24. Acne in males in this age group is more severe than in females. In those aged 25 to 34, the prevalence of acne drops to 8%, and in persons aged from 25 to 44, the prevalence is 3%. In these age groups, women have a higher incidence of acne. Although acne begins at puberty, it can affect anyone at any age.

Acne presents as different types of lesions. The condition is graded into four stages, based on the type and the number of lesions on one side of the face. These are summarized in Table 3-2.

The prevalence of acne decreases with increasing age.

Causes of Acne

Regardless of ethnic group, acne begins at the follicles and sebaceous glands. The difference in appearance between ethnic groups is a result of the skin's response to the condition. The major causes of acne seem to be genetic predisposition and hormonal changes. Family history has a role because people inherit their skin type. People with oily skin or oily/combination skin are more prone to develop acne.

Hormonal changes have their effect in the development of acne at the follicular and sebaceous gland level. At the follicular level, certain hormones, such as androgens—the hormone responsible for maleness—are found in lower quantities in females. They can cause the lining of the follicle to thicken and promote plugging. Androgens also stimulate and promote growth to the sebaceous gland, thus increasing the volume of oil released by the gland, further clogging the follicular channel. The pores close because of the increase in oil and the shedding of the follicle lining.

The lining of the follicle sheds cells that stick together and accumulate in the follicle and at the surface near the pore, forming closed comedones, or whiteheads. Blackheads, open comedones, form by the same mechanism, except that the pore stays open and the oil and dead skin oxidize and turn black. This black appearance is not related to dirt. (Figure 3-1 and Figure 3-2, next page).

Blackheads and whiteheads form by the same basic mechanism.

Sebum and dead skin cells also are magnets to attract bacteria that live in the pores. The natural defenses of the skin try to attack the bacteria. This weakens the follicular wall, which can rupture. The contents of the ruptured follicle empty into the

TABLE 3-2

The Four Stages of Acne

Stage 1: Mild

Comedones[*]—up to 10

Papulopustular lesions—up to 10

Inflamed cysts—none

Stage 2: Mild to Moderate

Comedones—10–25

Papulopustular lesions—10–20

Inflamed cysts—none

Stage 3: Moderate to Severe

Papulopustular lesions—20–30

Comedones—25–50

Inflamed cysts—a few

Stage 4: Severe

Papulopustular lesions—>30

Comedones—>50

Inflamed cysts—many

[*]Comedones include both whiteheads and blackheads.

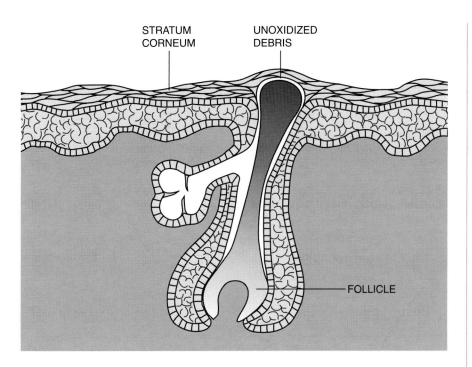

STRATUM
CORNEUM

UNOXIDIZED
DEBRIS

FOLLICLE

Figure 3-1

Whitehead

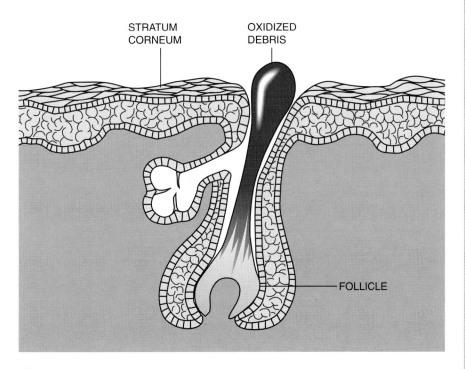

STRATUM
CORNEUM

OXIDIZED
DEBRIS

FOLLICLE

Figure 3-2

Blackhead

surrounding tissue of the dermis. This causes the body's natural defenses to react even more intensely. The skin swells and turns red, resulting in a deep-seated inflamed lesion that raises above the skin. This lesion is called a cyst.

Other causes of acne include physical irritation of the skin (acne mechanica) and prescription drugs, such as anticonvulsants, antidepressants, oral and topical steroids, birth control pills, contraceptives, and high doses of vitamin B.

Acne is also associated with mental and physical stress that affect hormonal changes. Worry about everyday problems or being under significant pressure at home or work can stimulate acne. Vigorous exercise can cause physical stress on the body, which can also cause hormones to change, leading to acne. Premenstruation is also a time of physical stress and hormonal change; acne outbreaks are common during this time.

Using skin and hair products that dry the skin excessively or that leave oily residues on the skin can also foment this condition. Prolonged sun exposure can irritate the skin and close the pores, and thus lead to acne. Although food is not directly related to acne outbreak, people react differently to different foods. Acne sufferers should watch what they eat and avoid foods that seem to cause acne outbreaks.

Acne is not caused by eating chocolate, French fries, hamburgers, potato chips, or other fatty foods. Nor is it caused by drinking sodas and carbonated beverages. It is not tied to sex in any way. Cosmetics can play a role in developing acne if the products are not appropriate to the person's skin type. Cosmetics should be chosen carefully with a view toward skin type and ingredients. It is best to avoid products that contain known allergens. Products labeled as noncomedogenic are less likely to irritate the skin and plug the pores.

As an oil gland and follicular problem, acne is most likely to occur in areas where these appendages are located, such as the face, chest, back, shoulders, and the buttocks. The average life of a pimple or pustule is 1 to 8 weeks. Because it is associated with genetic makeup and with hormonal activity, acne cannot be cured. The symptoms and artifacts of acne, however, can be treated.

Psychosocial and Emotional Impact of Acne

Although acne does not affect the sufferer's overall physical health or life span, the psychosocial impact of acne can be devastating emotionally and economically, to a point that it alters the quality of life of the affected individual. People suffering with severe acne are less likely to involve themselves in social activities. Those who have acne on their chest and back are less likely to wear swimsuits and are more likely to complain of pain during activities they do take part in.

Severe acne sufferers also have higher incidences of neuroses, low self-esteem, poor academic performance, anger, paranoid ideation, insomnia, hypersomnia, anorexia, hyperphagia, and social isolation. It is often the psychosocial impact of the condition that leads many people to seek medical attention. This does not mean that there is a direct correlation between the degree of the psychosocial dysfunction and the person's actual stage of acne. A person with stage 1 acne can feel he or she has a much worse case. Each person must be evaluated and treated as an individual based on his or her perception of the severity of the condition.

Adolescence is an especially critical time in an individual's psychosocial development. Acne at this stage of life can be exceptionally devastating to self-esteem. Because society is usually more critical of appearance in women than in men, this devastation to self-esteem is even greater in female teens. However, adults also suffer psychosocial impact in the workplace and at home. A misperception exists in some segments of society that adults with acne are socially, intellectually, and sexually immature.

Treatment of Acne

Health care professionals must attempt quick and intelligent treatment, both for the condition and its effects. Prompt and proper treatment of acne can decrease the frequency and severity of the person's current acne condition and can minimize scarring and recurrence of acne in the future.

Those with acne can view it as an emotional psychosocial problem.

Always obtain a medical history before treating a client with acne.

For best results, the health care practitioner should compile a complete health history of the individual, including an assessment of the person's general health, with a focus on kidney, liver, and gland functions; drug allergies; hair growth or loss; and previous acne treatments. The history should also include the duration of the condition as well as identifying points of execrations, such as premenstrual, seasonal, environmental, or other aggravating factors. The use of drugs, contraceptives, cosmetics, and skin and hair care products should also be assessed. The type of lesions and their number and location, as well as complications such as discoloration or scarring, should also be noted.

Acne can be treated both surgically and nonsurgically. Surgical treatments include intralesional injections with cortisone, comedonal extraction, and the excising and draining of lesions.

Nonsurgical treatments may be either topical or systemic. Topical treatments include the use of keratolytics, antibiotics, and salon skin care treatments with a variety of skin care products designed for use with acneiform skin. Keratolytics are agents that help normalize shedding of the follicular lining and remove dead skin cells from the follicle. Antibiotics help by killing or reducing the bacteria that release substances that promote inflammation and rupturing of the follicle.

Skin care treatments may be performed by licensed estheticians in a salon environment. These treatments include cleansing the skin, applying astringents, steaming, manual extraction, exfoliation of dead skin cells with enzymes, and using special products and machines designed to treat problem skin. These techniques are discussed in Chapter 4.

Systemic treatments include oral antibiotics, isotretinoin (Accutane), or with cases attributed to hormonal imbalance, hormone therapy. Oral antibiotics work by reducing or eliminating bacteria within the oil gland and the follicle. Isotretinoin, used for severe cases of acne, works by decreasing oil production at the gland, thus preventing the interaction between bacteria and the oil. It is this interaction that produces the irritating substances that cause the follicle to leak.

Hormonal therapy is indicated for people whose acne resists other forms of treatment and for those who are not good candidates for isotretinoin treatment. Hormonal therapy reduces oil production at the glandular level by preventing the gland from stimulating the production of oil by androgens. This treatment is suitable only for women, however, because it can cause female features in men from the decrease in androgens.

Medications for stage 1 and 2 acne can be obtained over-the-counter. Medications for more severe forms of acne require a doctor's prescription. In no case, though, should an esthetician suggest or prescribe even an over-the-counter medication. That should be done only by a physician. For *any* medication, the manufacturer's instructions should be followed and the results should be monitored carefully for signs of irritation that can make the acne condition worse. Table 3-3 lists the ingredients of some commonly used over-the-counter medications.

Oral antibiotics are commonly prescribed for the treatment of acne stage 3 and 4. Some antibiotics can cause a photosensitive reaction, which can leave the skin irritated and discolored.

The diagnosis of acne is the same in black skin and white skin. Skin care products and treatments are the same, but quite often the response to acne medications and treatments differ between black skin and white skin. Most acne products work by drying acne lesions. As a side effect, however, they also dry the noninvolved skin. This can lead to skin irritation and hyperpigmentation.

Facial treatments for black acneiform skin should be considered standard procedure. These treatments allow the skin to rebalance its pH, which is important in black skin to minimize unseen skin irritation and to exfoliate dull skin cells that can make the skin look gray, dull, discolored, and unhealthy. Manual extractions must be performed carefully in black acneiform skin. This step should be undertaken only after first preparing the skin with steaming.

Black acneiform skin should receive facial treatments as standard procedure.

Black skin is easy to irritate, but this is not usually noticed until some degree of damage has occurred. Irritation can cause pigmentary changes,

TABLE 3-3

**Common Over-the-Counter Acne
Medication Ingredients**

Benzyol Peroxide

Concentrations of 2.5%, 5%, and 10%

Works by killing the bacteria that promote acne and by
removing shedding cells from the follicle

Salicylic Acid

Concentrations of 0.5% and 2.0%

Works by removing shedding cells that promote follicular
plugging

Sulfur

Concentrations of 3.0% to 10%

Works by killing the bacteria that promote acne and
by removing shedding cells from the follicle

Sulfur/Resorcinol

Concentrations of 3.0% to 10.6%

Works by killing the bacteria that promote acne and
by removing shedding cells from the follicle

Glycolic Acid

Concentrations up to 10%

Works by removing shedding cells that plug the
pores

acne, eczema, and scarring. The health care professional should be attentive to signs of irritation, such as new dryness in isolated patches; peeling around the eyes, mouth, and the corners of the nose; a tight feeling on the skin; and itching and discoloration. Physicians should be even more attentive, looking for signs such as blanching under pressure, feelings of warmth, and raised textures. Acne medications and products for certain skin care treatments should have modified instructions on the frequency of use and possible side effects in black skin.

Acne cysts are quite frequently treated with intralesional steroids. Caution is necessary when using these medications with black skin, however, because permanent hypopigmentation can occur. Chemical peels are also used in the treatment of acne. These treatments work by exfoliating plugged follicles and decreasing scarring by resurfacing the skin. However, with black skin, strong acids like TCA (Trichloracetic acid) may be used with caution, but may cause scarring and hyperpigmentation. Dermabrasion is a common treatment for acne and acne scarring in white skin. In black skin, this technique can cause discoloration and scarring.

Chapter 4

Caring for Black Skin

S*kin requires constant care* to prevent problems that might become bothersome and to keep the skin healthy and looking and feeling good consistently. This requires a skin care regimen that is followed every day at home in addition to regular professional care and treatment in the salon.

SALON CARE

Salon-level skin care is conducted by licensed practitioners called estheticians, who are trained in all aspects of cosmetologic skin care. They are licensed to practice noninvasive skin care treatments, that is, they may work only on the surface of the skin and use no products that penetrate deeply into the skin. In addition to conducting effective skin treatments, they also offer advice on skin problems and recommendations on the value and proper use of the latest products and services.

Skin care services should be conducted in a commercial facility, such as a full-service beauty salon where the treatments are given in conjunction with other beauty services, or in special salons that provide only skin care services. Some dermatologists and other physicians who deal with skin problems also offer these services in their offices. In these cases, the treatments will still be given by a licensed esthetician. Estheticians who work with physicians are usually more highly trained and are allowed to be more aggressive in their treatments.

Although a great number of estheticians provide this level of care, relatively few have the training or experience to deal effectively with the care of black skin. For best results, the black consumer should seek care from those professionals who have the training and experience to recognize and respond to the special needs of black skin.

Black consumers should seek skin care from professionals who have experience in treating black skin.

THE FACIAL

Effective professional skin care starts with the facial, the most basic process in the salon. The properly administered facial treatment is the basis of the day-to-day work of the esthetician.

In its simplest terms, a facial is a multistep process designed to cleanse the client's skin, alleviate minor disorders, and normalize the skin's function. Properly given, the facial will also make the client feel good and enhance his or her feeling of well-being. A well-performed facial should take between 45 minutes and an hour, depending on the steps taken.

To give a facial properly, it is necessary to know the procedures, the equipment, and the products to use. It is also necessary to know how the skin functions and to be able to determine the client's skin type. The esthetician must have a thorough knowledge of skin structure and function and must understand what procedures accomplish and how they are followed. Knowledge, experience, and practice are of paramount importance. Equipment and products are also important.

A good facial can be given without using the specialized equipment developed for skin care; however, the proper equipment, properly used, makes the procedure more efficient and more effective. A skin care product of some type is always necessary—it is extremely important to use the right product for the client's skin type.

A facial has two parts: (1) deep pore cleansing, in which impurities are removed from the skin, and (2) normalization and treatment, in which nutrients and healing agents are put back into the skin. Because it performs both functions, the facial mask is a transition between the two parts. It continues and finishes the cleansing process and begins the normalization process.

One of the most important steps in the facial, however, begins before the esthetician actually starts working on the client. This is the consultation and analysis phase, in which the esthetician determines the client's skin type, examines the skin's condition, and decides on the proper course of treatment for that client. Once the esthetician has completed this analysis, the facial can begin with deep pore cleansing, the facial mask, and the normalization and treatment steps. The process is summarized in Table 4-1.

Consultation and Analysis

In this phase, the esthetician gathers the information about the client so that he or she can determine the proper course of action. The esthetician starts by asking the client a series of questions about health, dietary habits, lifestyle, skin care practices, and expectations about the facial.

Communication is the key to the success of the consultation, as the esthetician and the client develop a rapport. The esthetician learns about the client; at the same time, the client learns about the esthetician and develops confidence in the esthetician's ability and expertise. It is also the esthetician's opportunity to educate the client on skin care issues.

Good communication is a must for a successful consultation.

After gathering information, the esthetician moves the client from the office to the facial room, where the analysis phase begins. The esthetician examines the client's skin to determine its type and condition. After remov-

TABLE 4-1

The Facial Process

- **Consultation and Analysis**

  Determination of skin type

  Analysis of skin problems

  Decisions on course of
  treatment

- **Deep Pore Cleansing**

  Application of cleanser

  Rotary brushing

  Removal of cleanser

  Application of toner

  Massage

  Steaming

  Disincrustation

  Vacuum application

  Manual extraction

- **Facial Mask Application**

  Choice of mask type

  Application of mask

  Removal of mask

- **Normalization and Treatment**

  Iontophoresis

  High-frequency current

  Spray application of nutrients

  Application of moisturizer and treatment
  products

- **Posttreatment Consultation**

  Assessment of results

  Recommendations for continuing care

  Building of esthetician/client relationship

Note: Not all of these steps will be performed in every facial. Because each skin type requires different procedures, the steps will vary from facial to facial.

ing makeup and superficial dirt, the esthetician uses a magnifying lamp to check for blemishes, pore size, texture, and other obvious indications of skin condition. Next, the esthetician may use a Wood's lamp as a further check on the client's skin condition. This is an optional step.

A Wood's lamp (Figure 4-1) is a black (ultraviolet[UV]) light device, usually coupled with a magnifying lens. This device uses the principle that certain skin conditions fluoresce in different colors under black light. Table 4-2 summarizes Wood's lamp indications.

Figure 4-1
Wood's lamp

TABLE 4-2

Wood's Lamp Indications

Skin Type	Fluorescent Color
Normal	Blue-white
Dry	Light to deep purple
Dead cells	White
Clogged pores and blackheads	Orange
Dandruff	White

Deep Pore Cleansing

Deep pore cleansing removes dirt, excess sebum, and other impurities from the skin. In addition, ripe pimples and some other blemishes are extracted manually.

Cleanser Application. The first step in deep pore cleansing is the application of a cleanser suitable for the client's skin type. The cleanser is applied with the hands or with viscous sponges and worked into the skin with a rotary brush. If a rotary brush is not available, the cleanser may be worked into the skin with the hands. Figure 4-2 shows a rotary brush.

Brushing also gives a gentle, soothing massage that helps relax the client. For additional massage effect, the brushes can be used dry, although extended contact with dry brushes may cause irritation.

The rotary brush treatment typically is performed early in the facial process. Normally it is the first step after the analysis. However, it may be done after the steaming step.

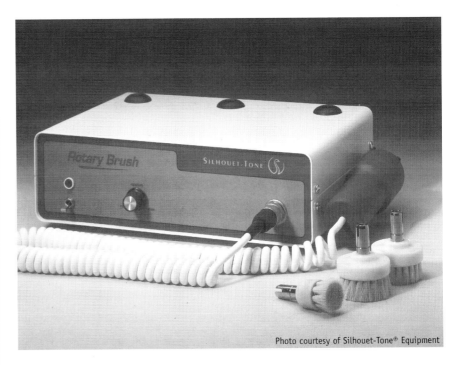

Photo courtesy of Silhouet-Tone® Equipment

Figure 4-2

Rotary brush machine

After brushing, the cleanser is removed with tepid water, and a toner or astringent is applied to remove all traces of the cleanser. After the cleanser is completely removed, the facial process moves to the massage phase. Cleanser application and removal should take 3 to 5 minutes

The brushes and other attachments should be cleaned with soap and hot water, then sanitized with alcohol. When not in use, they should be stored in an UV sterilizer or in a clean, dry, covered container or cabinet.

Massage. The facial massage is probably the most pleasant stage of the facial. It relaxes the client and helps prepare the skin for the steps that follow. It soothes and stimulates the skin and helps the skin rid itself of waste materials. Properly performed, the massage helps the body balance its energy. Good massage technique relies on a series of stroking, friction, kneading, and tapping movements, done in a smooth, firm, but gently, rhythmic manner. The movements are performed in a logical sequence. (See the section, More on Massage, later in this chapter.)

Massage is both a science and an art. As a science, it relies on knowledge of physiology and manipulation of energy fields. As an art, it relies on empathy, sensitivity, and an almost intuitive feel for the movements. Because of this, there is no one right way to give a good massage. There are almost as many techniques as there are practitioners. What the esthetician needs to remember is that it is more important to work in a logical sequence and to work rhythmically than it is to rely on mechanical adherence to rote procedures.

Clients enjoy the facial massage. Learn to do it well!

There is usually a learning curve for clients and it may be necessary for the esthetician to instruct the client on how to react to the massage and to tell him or her what to do and not do during the procedure. The client should be receptive, relax, and give in to the esthetician's movements. The client should concentrate on the massage and the sensations it produces and should try to forget worries. A fully relaxed client may fall asleep during the massage. This is an indication that the esthetician is doing everything perfectly.

The esthetician must be relaxed as well, concentrating on giving the massage and paying attention to the client's needs. The esthetician's state of mind will transmit itself to the client. The client will be able to sense the esthetician's mood and will react to that. The massage will not be a pleasurable event unless the esthetician radiates a mood of serenity and confidence.

Communication is vital. The esthetician should tell the client what will be done before the treatment and should encourage questions. Once the massage has begun, however, talking should be discouraged. Everything should be ready before the massage is started, so the esthetician does not have to fumble around for massage creams or essential oils or disrupt the rhythm.

The mood should be relaxed. Soothing music or special relaxation tapes should be played at a low volume. During an aromatherapy massage, the scent from the essential oils should also contribute to the mood. The room should be warm and comfortable; lights should be dimmed.

A small amount of massage cream should be warmed in the hands and gently applied to the client's face, smoothly and evenly. Initial contact with the face should be made firmly, but with light pressure. Pressure should be increased gradually. Once contact with the skin has been made, it should not be broken unnecessarily. If contact must be broken, the hands should be removed slowly, with pressure gradually diminishing until it is feather-light.

A massage should not be given if the client has a skin infection or skin disease. If the client has had cosmetic surgery within a year, the surgeon should be consulted and permission obtained before attempting the massage. Massage should be given carefully and sparingly if the client has high blood pressure or a heart condition or is pregnant. Stimulating maneuvers should not be used under these conditions. Movements, especially those in which moderate pressure is used, should be made in an upward direction to avoid pulling down the skin and promoting sagging. Pressure is usually applied with the middle, ring, and little fingers. The index fingers and thumbs are used only occasionally. The total massage should take 15 to 20 minutes.

Steaming. After the massage, the skin is steamed. Steaming offers a number of benefits. It expands the blood vessels and increases circulation. It softens the skin, loosens dead surface cells, and softens embedded dirt, oils, and blackheads. By relaxing the pores, steaming helps moisten and revitalize the skin. Equally important, it relaxes the client.

All traces of massage cream must be removed so the steam can penetrate. Steaming is allowed to continue for about 10 minutes. Essential oils may be added to the steam for their therapeutic or calming effects.

The steamer should be filled with distilled water. Ordinary tap water contains minerals that will form deposits in the machine and clog the nozzle. It takes at least 10 minutes for steam to start coming out of the nozzle once the machine is turned on, so it is necessary to start the machine well before the time it will be needed. While the machine is heating, the nozzle should be kept away from the client's face.

Steaming is usually accomplished with a vaporizer, a machine specially designed for the purpose. If the machine is not available, the same effects may be accomplished with a series of hot towel compresses.

Steaming can be relaxing for the client, especially if essential oils are used.

Disincrustation. The disincrustation step softens hardened sebum in the pores. It is accomplished with a machine that applies galvanic current to the skin (Figure 4-3, next page). The esthetician applies an alkaline disincrustation solution to the skin and helps it penetrate with the electric current. If the machine is not available, the step can be carried out with a series of cotton compresses soaked in the alkaline solution. This method is not as effective as using the galvanic current machine, however.

Disincrustation is only done on oily, blemished skin. It is not necessary to use this step on dry skin. This step should take 2 to 3 minutes.

Vacuum. The esthetician next uses the vacuum side of the vacuum/spray machine (Figure 4-4, next page) to remove excess oil and loose dirt from the skin. The machine works like a miniature vacuum cleaner and sucks up the dirt and debris. As with disincrustation, this step is only done on oily, blemished skin. This step should take 2 to 3 minutes.

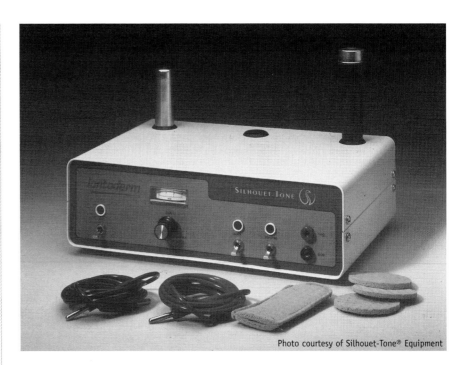

Photo courtesy of Silhouet-Tone® Equipment

Figure 4-3

Galvanic current machine

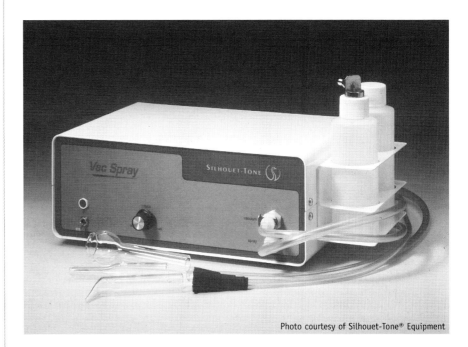

Photo courtesy of Silhouet-Tone® Equipment

Figure 4-4

Vacuum/spray machine

The vacuum treatment should be done after steaming and disincrustation when the pores have been opened and embedded oils have been softened. Except for very slight amounts of disincrustation solution or water, the skin should be free of any cleansers or lotions while it is being vacuumed. Any preparations on the skin will be sucked into the machine and may clog or otherwise damage it.

The vacuum nozzles, also called ventouses, should be cleaned with hot, soapy water and sanitized with alcohol. Then they should be stored in a dry sterilizer.

Manual Extraction. The skin is now ready for manual extraction, that is, the physical removal of blackheads, pimples, and other blemishes. The degree of manual extraction necessary varies according to the type of the skin and the degree to which it is blemished.

Manual extraction may be somewhat unpleasant for the client, but it is one of the most important parts of the facial. It is performed only on blemished skin.

Using the magnifying lamp, the esthetician gently removes blemishes with light to moderate pressure. Only the fingers, covered with cotton pads soaked in antiseptic, are used for this step. Metal or other instruments should never be used by an esthetician. Schaumburg extractors should be used only by qualified physicians. Once this step is finished, the esthetician will apply a mild antiseptic to the skin. It is important to avoid overdoing manual extraction in any single facial to prevent excessive discomfort to the client or possible damage to the client's skin. This step should not take more than 10 minutes. In many cases, it should be considerably less, depending on the individual client's tolerance and the degree to which the client's skin is blemished.

Manual extraction requires training and care. It should be done only by a properly trained and experienced esthetician, and only when it can be performed without using invasive procedures. It should never be attempted at home because disruption of the follicle can lead to more severe acne and skin bruising or dark spots.

Manual extraction requires special training and experience.

Facial Mask

The mask is a transition between the cleansing process and the normalization and treatment process, and performs some of the functions of both processes. There are many different types of masks. Depending on the type used, the mask can remove impurities from the skin, absorb excess oil, soothe or stimulate the skin, nourish the skin, or tighten the skin to remove small wrinkles temporarily. Because of the wide variety available, a competent esthetician can easily choose a mask suited to any client's particular needs.

Although each type of mask is applied according to its own characteristic requirements, there are some general techniques applicable to all masks. Regardless of type, it is necessary to follow the manufacturer's instructions. (See the section, More on Masks, later in this chapter.)

A small amount of the mask material should be removed from the jar with a spatula and placed on the back of the hand. The materials should never be taken from the container with the hands. Starting at the chin, a small quantity of the mask material is transferred from the back of the hand to the face with the fingers and spread evenly over the face. The mask is applied by spreading upward. The face should be covered thoroughly, but the mask should not be placed near the eyes or over the lips. The neck should also be coated with mask material.

The amount of time the masks are left in place varies with the type. In general, the hardening masks are left on slightly longer than soft masks because of the time needed for them to dry. The normal duration for a mask is 7 to 15 minutes although some may require a longer time. The esthetician should always monitor the client while the mask is working.

After the mask has done its work, it is removed. Some masks can be peeled off. Soft masks can usually be wiped off with moist cotton pads. Hard masks are usually softened with the application of a hot, damp towel, then wiped off with damp towels. Regardless of type, removal must be done carefully. Care must be taken not to stretch the skin while removing the mask. All mask material must be thoroughly removed. The total mask treatment, from application to removal, should take 10 to 20 minutes.

Normalization and Treatment

In this stage, the skin is nourished, revitalized, and protected. Cleansing has opened the skin to the environment and removed its surface oils and protective mantle. This stage puts nutrients back into the skin and provides protection from bacterial invasion until the skin's acid mantle regenerates.

Iontophoresis. Iontophoresis puts nutrients back into the skin. The process allows the penetration of water-soluble treatment products into the skin where they can work more effectively than they can by remaining on the surface. This step is accomplished with the same galvanic current machine used for disincrustation, except that the polarity of the current is reversed. In iontophoresis, the working electrode is set as the positive pole. The passive electrode is the negative pole. In this polarity condition, the skin is soothed and circulation decreased. Any desired treatment product can be used as long as it is water soluble and is on the acidic side.

A small amount of a water-soluble treatment product is lightly massaged into the skin, then the working electrode of the galvanic current machine is gently moved over the client's face so the product will penetrate. The client holds the passive electrode. The procedure is similar to that for disincrustation.

Unlike disincrustation, which is used only on oily, clogged skin, iontophoresis can be used on any type of skin. As before, however, the machine should not be used on pregnant women or clients with pacemakers, high blood pressure, or heart conditions. This step should take 2 to 3 minutes.

High-Frequency Application. The high-frequency machine (Figure 4-5, next page) increases circulation and helps the skin absorb treatment products and nutrients by stimulating the skin with high-frequency current. The current produces heat deep in the dermal layer of the skin. The ozone generated by the current also has germicidal properties and helps kill bacteria on the skin. In addition, the high-frequency current increases the absorption rate of skin creams.

> The steps of normalization and treatment nourish, revitalize, and protect the client's skin.

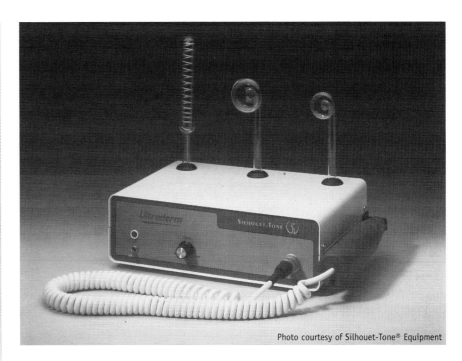

Photo courtesy of Silhouet-Tone® Equipment

Figure 4-5
Large high-frequency machine

The current can be applied directly by placing the electrode on the client's face. It may also be applied indirectly by having the client hold the electrode while the esthetician massages the treatment product into the skin. In addition, the electrode can be held a short distance away from the skin, producing a spark that helps promote healing. This step should take 2 to 3 minutes.

Spray Application. The spray has a number of purposes during the facial. After cleansing, it helps remove cleanser or massage cream. After manual extraction, it helps soothe the skin. At the end of the facial, it nourishes and refreshes the skin. Toners, astringents, or liquid treatment products suitable for the client's skin and for the result required may be applied with the spray attachment of the vacuum/spray machine, the electric pulverisator, or with a hand-pumped spray applicator.

The spray can be used at a number of points during the facial. This step should take about 1 minute.

Treatment Product Application. The last step of the facial is the application of a suitable treatment product, such as a moisturizer, oil absorber, or pH balancer. A small amount of the product is lightly massaged into the skin. This step should take about 1 minute.

Posttreatment Consultation

The end of the facial is not necessarily the end of the process. Once the client has changed into street clothes, the esthetician has an opportunity for a finishing consultation. This step is just as important as the rest of the process. Now, the esthetician can assess the treatment and answer any questions the client may have. This is also the time for the esthetician to outline the home treatment regimen for the client, suggest products for home use, and set up an appointment for the client's next facial.

PROFESSIONAL SKIN CARE EQUIPMENT

A good facial can be given without the use of specialized machinery. However, having and using the proper equipment makes the procedure more efficient and effective. A wide array of specialized machinery is available for professional skin care. Each type serves a different purpose.

Proper equipment is key to a successful facial.

There are a number of different manufacturers of skin care machinery. Many manufacturers provide the equipment as a package in self-contained racks. These racks hold the various pieces together and allow more efficient access to them during the facial. Regardless of the type of machinery, all manufacturers' instructions for proper use should be followed.

Facial Chair

A suitable treatment chair is the most important piece of equipment. It is the one piece of equipment that is used throughout the entire facial regardless of the length of the treatment or the number of steps involved. A comfortably padded, adjustable stool on casters for the esthetician is also important.

The chair should be sturdy and well padded so the chair is comfortable, and it should be upholstered with material that is easy to clean and

Figure 4-6
Facial chair

sanitize. The chair should be adjustable from fully upright to fully reclined, and the controls should be easy to work. When the chair is in the fully reclined position, the arm rests should be even with the padding.

It is important that the chair be as comfortable as possible because the client will be spending at least an hour in it during the facial. Comfort is the first step toward the relaxed feeling necessary to the success of the facial.

Magnifying Lamp

The magnifying lamp is used during skin analysis and manual extraction. Typically, the lamp consists of a circular fluorescent bulb around a four- to five-power magnifying lens. The lens and lamp assembly are attached to an articulating arm, so it can be moved to any desired position. Knobs on the arm lock the lamp into position.

During the facial, the lamp is placed very close to the client's face, so the bulb should be covered with a protective shield. If the light bothers the client, his or her eyes may be covered with moist cotton pads to shield them from the light.

Wood's Lamp

The Wood's lamp is a hand-held long-wave UV (black light) lamp with a magnifying lens and is used during the analysis. It must be used in a darkened room. Neither the client nor the esthetician should look directly into the Wood's lamp during the analysis. The client's eyes should be covered with moist cotton pads while using the lamp.

Rotary Brush

The rotary brush machine is used for deep cleansing, surface peeling, and light massage. These machines are available in a number of forms, ranging from hand-held portable units to floor units. Many units have speed controls to vary the brush speed. The detachable brushes come in a variety of sizes for use on different areas of the face or body. They are generally made from natural bristles and vary from coarse, for use on oily skin, to soft, for use on dry or mature skin.

Steamer

The steamer, also called a vaporizer, disperses steam onto the client's face. Steamers are available in a number of forms, ranging from free-standing floor models to small, portable units. Regardless of their configuration, however, they all have certain common features. They have a water reservoir, to hold the supply of distilled water; a heating element, to boil the water and produce steam; and a nozzle, usually on an adjustable arm, to direct the steam to where it is wanted.

Some models have a timer to measure the treatment time. Some models also have a removable felt ring around the nozzle, so that essential oils or other treatment substances can be placed on the felt ring to mix with the steam and be diffused over the skin.

Galvanic Current Machine

The galvanic current machine is a two-purpose device. It is used both for disincrustation and for iontophoresis, depending on the way the polarity of the machine is set. The machine generates an electrical current through two electrodes. One of the electrodes is the working electrode used by the esthetician; the other is the passive electrode held by the client.

In disincrustation, the working electrode is the negative pole; the passive electrode is the positive pole. In iontophoresis, the polarity reverses, so that the working electrode is the positive pole and the passive electrode is the negative pole.

In addition to the on-off switch, the galvanic current machine has a polarity reversing switch, a rheostat to regulate the amount of current, and an ammeter to measure the amount of current being delivered. As with any device that uses electric current, the manufacturer's instructions should be followed. The machine should not be used on pregnant women or on clients with certain medical conditions.

Vacuum/Spray Machine

Like the galvanic current machine, the vacuum/spray machine has two uses during the facial. The vacuum side is used to help remove excess oils and dirt from the skin, while the spray side is used to apply lotions or other skin care products in a fine, even mist.

The machine has a control to regulate the intensity of the suction or the spray volume to suit the client's needs. Accessories for the vacuum side include glass ventouses of different sizes. These are used for cupping different areas of the skin. The larger ventouses are used on the chin or forehead; smaller ventouses are used around the nose area.

The spray side of the machine is equipped with one or more bottles with fine mist spray nozzles. Although only one bottle can be attached to the machine at any one time, there is usually a quick-release mechanism so bottles can be interchanged rapidly. This lets the esthetician fill bottles with different solutions so the correct product can be used without emptying and refilling the spray bottle for each client.

The electric pulverisator, also known as the Dr. Lucas spray, is another type of spray machine. It is a hand-held device capable of combining herbs, herb teas, or essential oils with water and applying them in either a warm or cool spray. It has an internal water tank and two external containers made of glass. The glass containers are connected to the machine's spray nozzle with flexible tubing.

The tank is filled with distilled water, which then boils. The crushed herbs, teas, or other substances to be used for the treatment are placed in the larger glass container. The smaller glass container is used to catch any dripping. The spray starts when the flexible plastic tube is dipped into the large glass container. The material in the container is siphoned into the nozzle area where it mixes with the steam. The procedures for using the electric pulverisator are similar to those used for the spray machine. Care should be taken, however, because of the presence of boiling water.

High-Frequency Machine

The high-frequency machine generates a rapidly oscillating current that is transmitted to the client's skin through glass electrodes. In addition to the on-off switch, the machine has an intensity control to regulate the amount of current being applied, and an insulated electrode holder.

The electrodes are usually made of glass and come in a number of shapes. The most commonly used electrode is mushroom shaped. The electrodes are sealed and are filled with a gas, such as neon. When the electrode is inserted into the holder and current flows through it, the gas glows with a characteristic violet to reddish orange color. The same precautions taken with the galvanic current machine should be followed when using the high-frequency machine.

HOME SKIN CARE REGIMEN

The key to healthy, beautiful facial skin is proper cleansing to remove oil, dirt, makeup, dead surface cells, and other impurities that come to rest on and under it. The skin should be thoroughly cleansed at least twice a day—

once in the morning and once in the evening. Many people balk at twice daily cleansing, believing that it takes too much time. Nothing could be further from the truth! In reality, it takes less than 5 minutes to properly cleanse the face. This is a short time to spend to save a lot of time, trouble, and potential cosmetic difficulties later.

The process involves three major steps: cleansing, toning, and moisturizing. The skin care products used for each step should match the skin type—people with oily skin should use products formulated specially for oily skin; those with dry skin should use products formulated for dry skin; and those with normal skin should use products formulated for normal skin. This is an important consideration! No matter how good the product may be, if it is used on the wrong type skin, it will be ineffective at best, and potentially harmful at worst.

The products used for each step of skin care should match the person's skin type.

Step 1: Cleansing

Cleansing is the critical first step in the daily skin care process. This is the step in which dirt, grime, makeup, environmental pollutants, and other things that harm the skin are loosened and removed from the skin surface and the pores. It is important to use a good quality cleanser formulated for the specific skin type of the person using it.

Facial cleansers are pH balanced. This makes them preferable to soaps and detergents that are designed to be used on the rest of the body. If the pH of a cleansing product is not appropriate for the skin type, it can lead to excessive dryness, irritation, discoloration, or excessive oiliness that can lead to acne. This is especially a concern with black skin.

Unlike soaps, which are highly alkaline and tend to dry the skin and strip it of its acid mantle, facial cleansers are designed to cleanse the skin and the pores effectively, removing dirt and impurities without drying the skin or removing its protective oils.

Pour a small amount of cleanser on the hand and, starting at the neck and working upward, gently massage it into the face, using a circular motion. Work the cleanser into the skin, taking care not to exert downward pressure on the skin. Always stroke upward. After working the cleanser in thoroughly, rinse the face with copious amounts of tepid water. Never use hot water on the face. After rinsing with water, gently pat the skin dry with a clean, soft towel and apply the toner.

Occasionally, the skin should be exfoliated as part of the cleansing process. Exfoliation removes dead skin cells and helps the skin function properly. It also leads to healthier, more youthful-looking skin. Black skin, especially, gives off a wonderful radiant glow after exfoliation. This step is normally carried out two evenings a week, although the frequency can vary depending on the skin type and its condition.

Exfoliation should be part of the cleansing routine twice a week.

Exfoliation requires the use of a scrub in conjunction with the cleanser. Scrubs contain mild abrasive particles, which loosen and remove dead skin cells. The scrub formulation used should be based on the person's skin type.

First, cleanse the face with the cleanser. Rinse the cleanser off the skin with tepid water. Leave the face wet. Place a small amount of the scrub on the fingertips or on a clean, damp, cotton pad. Starting at the upper neck and working upward, gently massage the scrub on the skin, using short circular motions. Rinse the scrub from the skin with tepid water, pat it dry, and apply the toner.

Another part of the skin care cleansing regimen is the use of the facial mask. Commercially available masks for home use condition and moisturize the skin, giving the skin a soothing feel, with a smooth touch and healthy look. After toning, the mask should be applied two evenings a week, on evenings where the scrub is not used. Masks are discussed in greater detail later in this chapter.

After cleansing and toning, apply the mask to the face with smooth, upward strokes. Cover the face thoroughly, but do not cover the eyes or mouth. Let the mask dry for 15 to 20 minutes. Remove the mask by wiping with a wet towel. Make sure to remove all traces of the mask. Rinse the face with copious amounts of tepid water, pat the skin dry, and apply the moisturizer.

Step 2: Toning

Using a toner is the second step in proper cleansing of the skin. Toners remove cleanser residue. They also restore skin tone and correct imbalances in the skin. In addition, the toner helps restore the skin's acid mantle and protects the skin from bacterial invasion. Toning is important in the care of black skin because it helps to control excess oil in oily skin and helps soothe dry skin. Without taking this step, black skin tends to look dull, old, and discolored because of the buildup of soap residue. The residue has the effect of leaving a white film on a dark background, which gives the skin a gray appearance.

Toning for black skin helps control excess oil in oily skin and soothes dry skin. Do not omit this step!

Toners for dry and sensitive skin generally contain nonalcoholic ingredients. Astringents, toners for oily skin, generally have a high alcohol content.

To use the toner properly, pour a small amount on a cotton ball and gently apply it in a small circular motion starting at the upper neck and moving up the face to the forehead. Use only light pressure. Lightly rinse the excess toner from the skin with tepid water and pat the skin to remove excess water.

During the toning process, oil and dead skin cells continue to be removed from the skin surface. Cells that are removed from black skin can sometimes leave dark deposits on the cotton ball, leading the user to think their face is still dirty. As a result, they may continue toning until the cotton ball stays clean and overtones the skin. Do not repeat this step more than three times. Overtoning may irritate the skin and cause dryness and discoloration. After toning, the skin is ready for the moisturizer.

Step 3: Moisturizing

The last step in the daily skin care regimen is moisturizing, a process that provides nourishment and water to the skin. The cleansing process has opened the skin to the environment and removed its surface oils as well as dirt and other impurities. The toner has helped restore the skin to its normal state. It is the job of the moisturizer to complete the process and normalize the skin's functioning.

Moisturizers are generally emulsions that contain oil and water. They are designed to help prevent dryness, itching, discoloration, and to make the skin look, feel, and work better. There are different kinds of moisturizers. *Protective moisturizers* contain humectants and other ingredients that trap moisture in the skin and keep it moist. Skin dries out when water is lost through evaporation to the environment, when the humidity is low, or when the skin's natural protective barriers have been breached. All of these conditions interrupt the skin's ability to prevent water loss. This is the most common role for a moisturizer. As a result, protective moisturizers represent the largest class of this kind of product.

A moisturizer provides nourishment and water to the cleansed and toned skin.

Therapeutic moisturizers contain ingredients that help heal and soothe the skin. They penetrate the skin and affect its function and structure. *Cosmetic moisturizers* contain pigments and ingredients that hide skin defects. They help alter the appearance of the skin, but do not penetrate the skin, nor do they have any effect on its function or structure.

As with any skin care product, regardless of the function of the moisturizer, it must be matched to the skin type of the person using the product.

Black skin has a unique perceptual concern with moisturizers. It is a common misperception that black skin produces more oil than white skin. As discussed in Chapter 1, this is not true. It is true, however, that black skin sometimes looks oily when a moisturizer is applied. This is due only to the fact that any oil stands out more when placed on a dark background. The darker the skin, the more the oil in the moisturizer will be visible.

Apply the moisturizer to the still damp, but not wet, skin. Use the product sparingly. A little bit goes a long way. Put a pea-sized dab of the moisturizer on the fingertips and gently massage it into the skin, starting at the neck and working upward. Use circular motions while taking care not to exert downward pressure on the skin.

Although not the most important part of the skin care process, the massage is often the most memorable phase. Touch works wonders. As a result, the massage is the most emotional part of the process and the part of the process that does most to forge the link of confidence and trust between the client and the esthetician.

The massage is often the most memorable part of skin care.

Types of Massage

There are many types of massage. Some are based on body structure, that is, on the manipulation of muscle tissue, bones, and connective tissue, to achieve the therapeutic goal. Others are based on energy, on the manipulation of the life force of the body to achieve the therapeutic goal. Both use physical manipulation of one kind or another. Many of these massage techniques are valuable in the practice of esthetics.

The techniques of most interest to the esthetician are Swedish massage, shiatsu massage, acupressure, reflexology, aromatherapy massage, and lymphatic drainage massage. The esthetician often combines elements from all of these to deliver the most effective and beneficial massage to the client.

Swedish massage is a structure-based system in which deep muscle tissues are manipulated by a series of kneading, slapping, or rubbing strokes that affect both deep and superficial muscles and the joints. It stimulates circulation, improves muscle tone, and relieves soreness.

Shiatsu massage is an energy-based system of massage that involves pressure on acupressure points along the body's energy meridians, combined with stretching of the spine and limbs. It regulates and balances the energy flow of the body's organs.

Acupressure massage is similar to shiatsu and follows the same principles. The only difference between the two is that acupressure relies solely on pressure point manipulation. It also is an energy regulator and balancer.

Reflexology is an energy-based system of therapeutic massage that manipulates areas on the hands and the soles of the feet to achieve balance in the inner organs. The principle behind reflexology is that reflex points in the hands and feet correspond to various organs.

Aromatherapy massage is a structure-based system that uses essential oils along with the body manipulation. During the manipulations, the essential oil penetrates and affects the organ underlying the point of manipulation.

Lymphatic drainage massage is a structure-based system that uses gentle strokes and pressure along the lymphatic channels that lie just under the skin. The purpose of lymphatic drainage is to speed the passage of toxic waste materials through the lymphatic system to rid the body of toxins more rapidly.

Benefits of Massage

Massage provides a number of physical and psychological benefits. Physically, it affects almost every system of the body; psychologically, it brings relaxation and a tremendous sense of well-being to the client.

Massage helps the body cope with the stresses of the environment by relieving the tensions of daily life. Thus, the body uses its natural energy more productively.

The benefits of massage seem almost endless!

Massage also helps the body feed. It improves the circulation of the blood throughout the body, increasing the amount of nutrients and oxygen delivered to the cells, tissues, muscles, bones, and organs. It lets blood return to the heart more easily, thus reducing its exertions.

By cleansing the body, massage removes waste products, increases the efficiency of the liver, and increases lymphatic flow. Massage helps cleanse the blood and helps restore normal breathing patterns.

Massage soothes the body and sedates the nervous system, thereby releasing endorphins, the natural pain killers of the body. It reduces muscular tension and relieves fatigue by eliminating lactic acid that builds up in muscles after exertion. It relaxes muscle spasms and breaks down adhesions in the tissues. It also lowers blood pressure.

Massage tones the body. Although it cannot replace exercise, massage can restore tone to flaccid muscles. It increases the flexibility of joints and muscle size.

Massage revitalizes the body by balancing the nervous system and bringing the energy flow of the body into balance. It increases the level of energy and helps the body heal itself. Once the body is healed, massage lets it stay well by maintaining a level of health and vitality in the body.

Massage beautifies the body by improving the texture and appearance of the skin. It softens the skin and loosens and removes dead surface cells. By toning the facial muscles, it helps reduce wrinkles and prevent sagging. By improving circulation, it brings color to the face.

Massage helps recontour the body. It helps eliminate the fat deposits sometimes known as cellulite. It also helps maintain correct posture and balance. Because a high level of health and vitality are being maintained, all systems are in balance and clients feel good about themselves. This good feeling promotes the body's natural beauty.

There is a link between the physical aspects of massage and the psychological aspects. Emotions are retained in the cells, just as tensions are retained in the muscles. Emotions can be massaged away just as tensions are. Relaxation is a psychological state of mind as well as a physical state of body. In addition, the communicative aspects of touch, the physical contact between two people, adds its own psychological impact to the massage experience. Massage reduces mental fatigue as well as muscle fatigue.

Physical Manipulations of Massage

The physical basis of massage is manipulation of both superficial and deep muscle tissue delivered to the client in a series of rhythmic strokes, stretching movements, and the application of pressure at selected points on the body.

Stroking (Effleurage). Stroking, or effleurage, is the most basic and the most used movement in the massage. The movements are done with only light to moderate pressure. Work over an area of the body begins with gentle stroking, which gradually becomes more firm and finishes up as gentle stroking again.

Stroking movements induce relaxation and sedate the nervous system. All stroking movements are done slowly

Stroking movements are important in the massage for inducing relaxation and sedating the nervous system.

and rhythmically. The wrists are loose and flexible and the hands are relaxed. The movements are controlled by the arm and upper body muscles. Gentle stroking is done by gliding the hands over the body in broad, long movements. Friction is kept to a minimum.

Feathering is the lightest touch of stroking. It is used to break contact with the body, to avoid the unpleasantness of a sudden loss of touch between the client and the esthetician. Feathering requires an extremely light touch, with the hands just lightly brushing the body.

Regardless of the pressure used, stroking is done in one direction only. The movement does not go back and forth over an area but moves around it in broad circles.

Friction. Friction uses heavier pressure than stroking. The hands apply light pressure before starting to move, then they move back and forth over the area, with pressure gradually building from light to heavy. Friction increases circulation and promotes warmth in the deeper muscle tissues. These movements are soothing. As with stroking movements, friction should be controlled by the arm and upper body muscles with the wrists and hands relaxed and flexible.

Petrissage. Petrissage movements involve kneading, wringing, pulling, and rocking motions and are used to massage the deeper muscle masses of the limbs and fleshy areas of the body. These maneuvers relax deep muscle tissue while stimulating the skin. They also increase circulation and promote waste removal from the tissues. They tone and firm weak muscles. Petrissage is very good for oil dry skin because it stimulates sebum production. All of the varieties of petrissage are accomplished with a rhythmic hand-to-hand alternation of pressure and release.

Tapotement. Tapotement movements involve various forms of percussion, including hacking, clapping, pummeling, tapping, and pinching. Tapotement movements are stimulating to the body. They tone muscles and the skin and improve circulation. Hacking, clapping, and pummeling are used only on the fleshy areas of the body and are never used on the face. Hacking uses the edges of the little fingers and the hands; clapping uses the cupped palms; pummeling uses the fleshy sides of the clenched fists. The hands and wrists are relaxed. The hands are bounced rapidly in alternating strokes up and down the muscle areas being worked on. The pressure should be heavy enough to stimulate the muscles, but not so heavy that they cause pain.

Vibration. Vibration is a rapid shaking movement of muscle tissue and can be either soothing or stimulating. It can be used to stimulate organs directly below the muscle tissue and is suitable for use on the face to stimulate the more fleshy areas. Vibratory motion is accomplished by rapidly contracting and relaxing the muscles of the forearm. For soothing vibrations, the entire relaxed hand is placed on the muscle tissue and vibrated. For stimulating vibrations, only the fingertips are used. This gives motion much like a mechanical vibrator.

Stretching. Gentle stretch maneuvers relieve tightness, improve flexibility in the joints, and are soothing and relaxing. The joint should be moved through its full range of motion, first in one direction, then in the other. Although the joint should be stretched through its full range, care must be taken not to force the movement. Stretching movements are mostly done on the neck, wrists, and ankles as well as on the large joints, such as the hips, pelvis, and shoulders.

Pressure. Finger pressure is applied to pressure points, or tsubos, along the meridians to remove energy blockages. It is also applied to sensitive

areas in the muscles to relieve tightness. The amount of pressure applied varies from light to heavy, although it should never be heavy enough to cause pain. The fingers should remain relaxed while applying pressure, with the force coming from the weight of the body.

The pressure used during massage should *never* cause pain!

The pressure may be applied rhythmically by gradually increasing and decreasing the pressure as the fingers remain still. Or it may be applied while moving the fingers in a circular or zigzag motion over the area, moving the underlying tissues but not sliding over the skin.

Although the body has many pressure points, the esthetician will work mostly with those on the head and face, along with a few points on the hands, arms, and legs. All of the points lie along a meridian, as shown in Figures 4-7 and 4-8. Controlled pressure to these points relieves tension, eases fatigue, and removes energy blockages, all of which help clear the skin and improve its functioning.

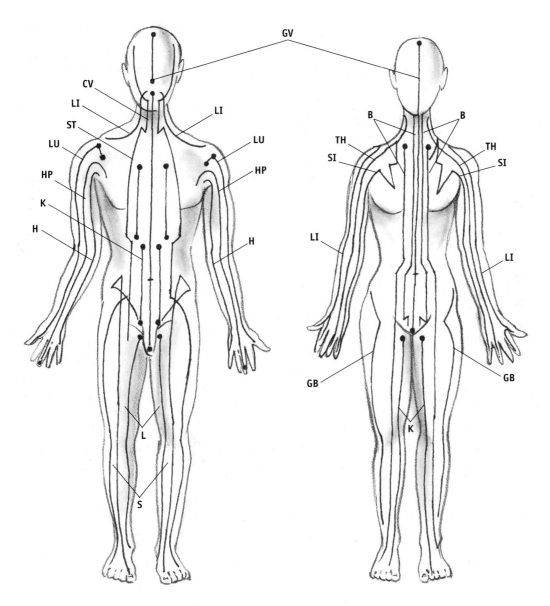

Figure 4-7
Meridians

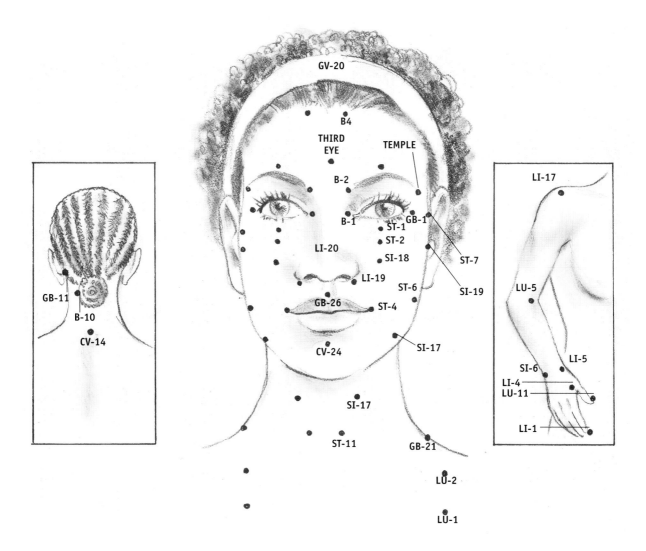

Figure 4-8

Major pressure points

On the bladder meridian (B), B-1 relieves tired eyes. B-2 relieves bloodshot eyes. B-4 relieves headache and clears sinuses. B-10 relieves headache and eyestrain.

In the conception vessel (CV), CV-24 helps smooth wrinkles below the lips.

On the gallbladder meridian (GB), GB-1 helps remove wrinkles around the eyes. GB-11 helps relieve dizziness. GB-21 relieves tension at the shoulders.

In the governor vessel (GV), GV-14 helps relieve tension in the neck, helps clear blemishes, and helps relieve migraine headache. GV-26 helps smooth wrinkles around the nose and lips.

On the large intestine meridian (LI), LI-1 helps remove blemishes. LI-4 helps relieve eye fatigue and headache and helps remove blemishes. LI-5 helps relieve pain in the wrist. LI-17 helps improve circulation. LI-18 helps improve respiration. LI-19 helps remove wrinkles around the nose and lips. LI-20 helps open sinuses.

On the lung meridian (LU), LU-1 helps relieve congestion in the chest. LU-2 helps relieve tension in the shoulders. LU-5 helps improve circulation in the arm. LU-11 helps relieve fatigue in the throat and vocal chords.

On the small intestine meridian (SI), SI-6 helps relieve facial blemishes and boils. SI-17 helps relieve sore throat. SI-18 helps tone cheek muscles to prevent sagging and helps ease facial swelling. SI-19 helps relieve headache and dizziness.

On the stomach meridian (ST), ST-1 helps remove bags beneath the eyes. ST-2 helps remove bags beneath the eyes and helps relieve eye fatigue. It also helps clear blemishes. ST-4 helps remove wrinkles around the nose and lips. ST-6 helps relieve tension in the lower jaw. ST-7 helps tone cheek muscles to avoid sagging cheeks. ST-11 helps relieve tension in the neck.

In addition to these meridian points, a number of other pressure points are important to estheticians. The "third eye" helps relieve tension and headache, helps clear sinuses, improves circulation, and restores color to the complexion. The pressure points on the temples help relieve headache. There are also a number of pressure points on the bony protuberances around the perimeter of the eye sockets.

MORE ON MASKS

Facial masks are a transition step between cleansing the skin and normalizing its functions. Depending on its type, a mask will remove impurities from the skin, absorb oils, tighten, nourish, soothe or stimulate the skin. Facial masks are one of the world's oldest beauty aids. Since antiquity, women have used clays, muds, and creams on their faces to cleanse and tone their skin. Many of these substances are still being

Facial masks have been used for hundreds, perhaps thousands, of years.

used. Today, a vast number of masks are commercially available for use at home. In addition, it is possible to make effective masks from items found in the kitchen.

Masks can be placed into two categories: hard or tightening masks and soft or conditioning masks. Most tightening masks are applied as a paste, which dries and hardens. The primary action occurs during the drying phase. Most conditioning masks are applied as a soft, moist paste and do not dry. The primary action occurs because of the active ingredients in the mask. Masks that harden are more difficult to remove than soft masks.

Hardening masks are generally used for cleansing and for toning up skin. They are most often used with normal to extremely oily skin types. Soft masks are generally used to nourish and normalize skin and are most often used with normal to extremely dry and mature skin types. Any given facial mask, however, may perform both hard and soft mask functions.

Tightening masks improve skin tone and texture and temporarily remove wrinkles and fine lines. They also refresh the skin. As the mask is applied, it has an initial cooling effect because of its moisture content. This cooling effect soothes the skin, which has just undergone a thorough cleansing. As the moisture evaporates, the materials in the mask form a film, which contracts as it dries, thus tightening the skin. At the same time, since the mask does not let the skin breathe, perspiration and sebum are kept from escaping and stay in the skin. This plumps up the skin. As a consequence, wrinkles and fine lines are removed, although this effect lasts only a relatively short time.

Excess oils, dead surface cells, and dirt, which have been loosened by the previous cleansing procedures, are absorbed by the mask material to provide additional cleansing. In addition, the action of the mask stimulates the circulation of blood in the blood vessels closest to the surface. This increased blood flow brings additional oxygen and nutrients to the skin. When the mask is removed, the skin has a radiant glow; it feels tighter, it looks better, and the person feels better.

Conditioning masks, which can include some tightening masks that have active ingredients added, nourish the skin. They add vitamins and minerals to the skin, in addition to increasing the circulation. Some active ingredients help fight blemishes and soothe irritations and reduce inflammation. Others draw out impurities, while still others add moisture to the skin surface.

A mask should be chosen that fits the skin type and that accomplishes the effect intended. Commercially available masks can be classified into a number of types. Their ingredients may vary, but there is a wide overlap in the functions performed by the different types. Before using any type of mask, test it on a small area of the skin to make sure the client has no allergic reaction.

Algae masks nourish and remineralize the skin and are excellent for use on dry and normal skin. This type of mask should not be used on people who are allergic to shellfish.

Clay/mud masks absorb oil, draw impurities, and tighten the skin. These masks are good for use on oily skin. With the addition of active ingredients such as sulfur, camphor, or certain herbs, they are also good for use on blemished skin.

Collagen masks are supermoisturizing masks that add moisture to the skin and help smooth fine lines and wrinkles. They are excellent for use on dry or dehydrated skin and are especially beneficial for mature skin.

Contour masks firm and tighten the skin and temporarily remove fine lines and wrinkles. They are suitable for use on most skin types but should not be used on couperose areas or on sensitive skins. These masks are extremely difficult to use and should only be applied by well-trained and qualified estheticians.

Cream masks are available in many different formulations, depending on their active ingredients. Most contain emollients, herbal extracts, and minerals for softening, nourishing, and moisturizing the skin. These are generally designed for use on dry, mature, and sensitive skins. Some are medicated, containing antiseptics and healing agents for soothing and healing the skin and fighting blemishes. These are generally designed for use on oily, blemished skins.

Paraffin masks are used to tighten the skin and temporarily remove fine lines and wrinkles. They may be used on any type of skin except couperose and sensitive skins, but work best on dry and mature skins. Like contour masks, paraffin masks are difficult to use and should be applied only by a qualified esthetician.

Wheat germ masks are used on all types of skin to nourish and revitalize it. They make excellent secondary masks, used for nourishing the skin after another type of mask is used.

Masks are applied after the cleansing and toning steps are completed and skin is most receptive to the benefits of the mask. Although each type of mask differs in its application, in general, they are spread over the face, avoiding the eyes. They remain on the face for a specified amount of time, then removed. In all cases, the manufacturer's instructions should be followed.

In addition to those masks that are commercially available, effective nourishing masks may be made from a wide variety of fruits and vegetables. Most fruits and vegetables contain high levels of vitamins and nourish the skin. Acidic fruits such as strawberries, plums, grapefruit, and oranges are astringent and are good for use on oily skin. Lemons may be too acidic and should be diluted in water before using. Other fruits, such as avocados, apricots, bananas, and peaches, are soothing and moisturizing and are most suitable for use on dry skin. Papaya and pineapple contain enzymes that help dissolve dead surface cells and remove surface impurities.

Common household fruits and vegetables can be formulated into facial masks.

Vegetables suitable for homemade masks include cucumbers, carrots, potatoes, spinach, and tomatoes. Cucumbers and potatoes are both hydrating and oil absorbing and are suitable for oily and dry skin. Carrots are hydrating and soothing and are best used on oily skin. Spinach is also good on blemished skin. In general, acidic fruits and vegetables are best used on normal to oily skin; nonacidic fruits and vegetables are best used on normal to dry skin.

Many of the herbs found in the home kitchen may be made into strong teas or poultices for use as home facial masks. These include fennel and celery seeds, which are soothing and cleansing; parsley and sage, which are astringent; rosemary and peppermint, which are stimulating and refreshing; and sesame and thyme, which are soothing and softening. Other herbs of value include aloe vera, comfrey, and chamomile.

Other products found in the kitchen are also beneficial when used on the skin. These include wheat germ, oatmeal, and brewer's yeast, which are nourishing and cleansing and can also be used as a base to carry fruit and vegetable pulps and herb teas. Yogurt and buttermilk soften and cleanse as well as nourish. Egg whites are tightening; egg yolks are nourishing and soothing. Honey is a natural moisturizer. Vinegar, especially cider vinegar, helps normalize skin functioning and restores the acid mantle of the skin. It is also astringent, yet can help soften skin.

To use as facial masks, mash fruits and vegetables to a pulp. Use them in that form or mix with a small quantity of light vegetable oil or with wheat germ, brewer's yeast, or oatmeal to make a paste. Apply pulps with a runny consistency over gauze to keep the mess to a minimum. Make herbs into a tea and apply to the skin with cloth compresses. Leave the mask on the face for 5 to 10 minutes, then remove with a damp, soft cloth or cotton pad. After removing the mask, rinse the skin thoroughly with lots of tepid water, then gently pat the skin dry.

When making masks from fruits, vegetables, herbs, or other kitchen items, be careful. Avoid products known to cause allergic reactions. If an allergic reaction occurs, discontinue use immediately.

SANITATION AND SAFETY IN THE SALON

In a salon, cleanliness is of paramount importance, whether working on the skin, working on the hair, working on the nails, or applying makeup. Proper sanitary procedures are vital for controlling harmful bacteria and preventing disease.

The bacteria of concern include the *bacilli,* the *cocci,* and the *spirilla,* which derive their names from their shapes. The bacilli, the most numerous, are rod shaped. Many have flagellae for locomotion. These bacteria are responsible for diseases such as tetanus and influenza (Fig. 4-9, next page).

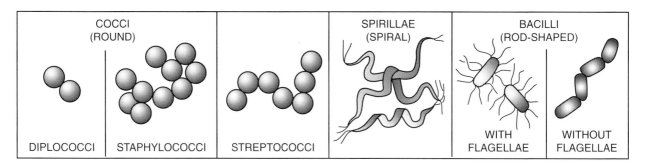

Figure 4-9
Bacterial Shapes

The cocci are round bacteria that grow in pairs, *diplococci,* in chains, *streptococci,* or in clusters, *staphylococci.* They are largely nonmotile. Diplococci are responsible for diseases such as pneumonia; streptococci for infection, for example, the "strep throat;" and staphylococci for pus-forming infections, such as boils and abscesses. The spirilla are motile, spiral-shaped bacteria.

Bacteria are not the only disease-causing organisms of concern to the esthetician. Like most pathogenic bacteria, viruses are infectious parasites. *Viruses,* however, are not living organisms and can only exist and reproduce inside living cells. *Virions,* the name given to virus particles, are submicroscopic, ranging from one quarter the size of a single bacterium to much smaller. They can be seen under the electron microscope. Each virion consists of a protein shell surrounding a core of nucleic acid, which may be either deoxyriboneucleic acid (DNA) or ribonucleic acid (RNA).

DNA-viruses are responsible for such diseases as herpes simplex, venereal herpes, shingles, and some tumors. This type also causes warts. RNA-viruses are responsible for such diseases as measles, mumps, polio, meningitis as well as the common cold. DNA-viruses reproduce in the nuclei of living cells; RNA-viruses reproduce in the cell cytoplasm.

Sanitation

The practice of proper sanitation is vital to the success of the salon. The salon must be kept spotlessly clean, as must the implements used by the esthetician. The esthetician must wear clean clothing and make sure that his or her hair and body are clean. Hands should be washed with soap and hot water and sanitized with alcohol before beginning work on a client. Wherever possible, disposable materials should be used.

Sanitation has two phases: *sterilization,* killing existing bacteria and viruses, and *prevention,* keeping new germs from growing. Towels and smocks, for example, must be washed in detergent and hot water and then be stored in a closed, dry area. Implements must be washed in hot, soapy water and rinsed or wiped with alcohol after use and then be stored in a dry sanitizer, a closed cabinet containing a fumigant or a UV light source (Fig. 4-10).

Sterilization in the salon may be accomplished through the use of heat, UV light, or chemicals. Heat may be moist, as in boiling or steaming, or dry, as in baking. High heat is effective in killing germs, but it may have an

Know and practice the two phases of sanitation!

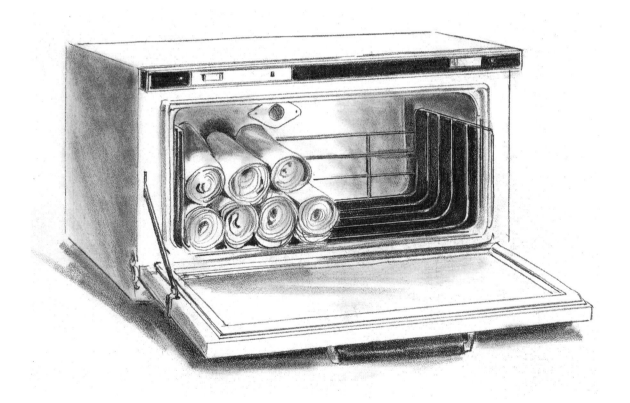

Figure 4-10
Dry sanitizer

adverse effect on many implements, especially those made of plastic. Short-wave UV light is effective in killing germs and is used in commercially available dry cabinet sanitizers and industrial germicidal lamps.

Chemical sterilizing agents include fumigants, antiseptics, and disinfectants. *Fumigants* are chemical fumes that have the ability to kill germs. *Antiseptics* and *disinfectants* are liquid or dry chemical germicides. They differ only in degree. Antiseptics are generally milder than disinfectants and can be used safely on the skin. Isopropyl alcohol (99%), boric acid, hydrogen peroxide (3%), sodium hypochlorite (bleach), and some soaps are commonly used antiseptics. Quaternary ammonium compounds (quats), formaldehyde, ethyl alcohol (70%), cresol, and phenol are commonly used disinfectants. Formaldehyde has been a popular disinfectant for salon use. Recent evidence, however, suggests that it is a powerful carcinogen and should not be used. Many state boards are considering a ban on formaldehyde or formaldehyde derivatives.

Consult your state cosmetology board and local health department for recommendations on safe and effective germicides for use in the salon. Manufacturers' instructions for commercial germicides should be followed.

Prevention of Infectious Diseases

The prevention of infectious diseases should be at the top of the salon professional's mind. Never work on a client who has an obvious infectious disease. Instead, refer that client to a physician. As a matter of good professional practice, wash and sterilize all equipment used during a facial and promptly discard disposable materials in a covered waste receptacle.

It is also necessary to be aware of diseases that may not be readily evident, including acquired immunodeficiency syndrome (AIDS). The AIDS virus is transmitted through blood or other body fluids, usually either through sexual contact or sharing of needles. According to the Centers for Disease Control and Prevention, the chance of transmission of AIDS by any other means is small.

Although the risk may be small, workers may want to consider using latex rubber gloves, even though the sense of touch may be slightly diminished.

Safety

Safety should also be a key concern in the salon. During the course of a facial, an esthetician comes in contact with heat, water, steam, and electricity. Heat and steam pose burn hazards; water can cause slipping, electricity can be a shock hazard. It is necessary to keep both the client and the worker safe.

Safety is largely a matter of awareness—of being safety conscious and using common sense. It is also a matter of good housekeeping. Spills should be wiped up as soon as they occur, before anyone can slip and fall. Trash and debris should not be allowed to accumulate, but should be disposed of promptly. Vaporizers and other heat

Be aware of all safety concerns in your salon. Heat, steam, water, and electricity pose significant hazards if used improperly.

sources should be monitored closely when they are being used so the client does not get burned. Lights should be covered to cut glare and as protection if the bulb should break. Passageways should be uncluttered to prevent accidents. Electrical circuits should not be overloaded. Electrical machinery should be kept away from water to prevent short circuits.

The Occupational Safety and Health Act (OSHA) applies just as much to salons as it does to other manufacturing and service businesses. OSHA is responsible for ensuring safety in the workplace. The agency that administers OSHA has the authority to conduct inspections of any business location and to levy fines for noncompliance with safety regulations. Salon owners and managers are required by law to maintain a safe working environment for their employees. Check with the local OSHA office to get information on regulations and to get advice on compliance with the rules.

Chapter 5

Black Hair and Nail Care

Poets and writers have often referred to hair as "the crowning glory" of the human body. It is one of the most prominent appendages of the body, and quite possibly, the appendage given the most attention. In fact, though, hair has no particular function other than decoration, yet its care and styling generates and continues to support a multibillion dollar industry.

Just as black skin requires special considerations in treatment and grooming, so does black hair. Black hair is naturally curly. It is also very prone to dryness, dullness, breakage, and scalp irritations. In addition, fast-changing fashion trends expose hair to many styles and products that can damage it. Therefore, black hair must be styled in certain ways and hair care products specially formulated for black hair used.

Hair care is a growth industry and represents a multibillion dollar market. The retail market for ethnic hair care products has reached as high as $1.7 billion and is still on the rise. The majority of these products are sold to black consumers in the United States. Considering that African-Americans make up only 12% of the population of the United States, the potential world market for ethnic hair care products is truly staggering. In Africa alone, for example, there are more than 650 million people. Numbers such as these require that skin care professionals as well as consumers have the knowledge necessary to choose the right products and to properly care for this psychologically vital appendage.

HAIR AND THE BODY

In humans, hair grows from below the skin everywhere on the body except on the palms of the hands and the soles of the feet. There are two types of hair—Vellus hair and terminal hair.

Vellus hair is also referred to as baby hair, although it grows on adults as well as children. It is very short, less than 30 microns in length; very fine, less than 40 microns in diameter; and hypopigmented, that is, colorless. Vellus hair grows virtually everywhere on the body in both women and men. Because of its extremely small length and diameter and lack of coloration, however, it is often difficult to see.

Terminal hair is coarse and is found on the scalp, the underarms, and the pubic areas in women and men. Terminal hair also grows on the arms, legs, chest, back, and face of men. On average, a person whose scalp and hair are healthy will grow hair at a rate of half an inch per month.

Hair Growth

Hair growth is a genetic characteristic. Hair length, amount, color, texture, and pattern are determined at birth and are related to family traits. Cutting hair has no effect whatsoever on its growth. The average adult human scalp contains 100,000 to 350,000 hair follicles and the average person sheds 100 to 150 hairs per day. This hair loss by a healthy person is normal and is replaced with new hair without the lost hair ever being missed.

Hair growth depends on one's genetic characteristics. Cutting has no effect on hair growth.

Hair grows below the skin in the hair bulb, which rests in the hair follicle (Figure 5-1). Here, hair is produced from the multiple growth of specialized cells that line the inner hair follicle at its root. This area is constantly fed by the blood supply from the hair papilla, which is an extension of the dermis. As the cells germinate in the hair bulb, they come together to form a solid structure.

Hair growth is not a continuous process. Hair follicles undergo three separate, alternating phases of existence—the anagen, the catagen, and the telogen. Growth occurs only in the anagen phase. The anagen phase is longer for scalp hair than for body hair. This phase also lasts longer in women than in men.

As growth slows, follicles begin to atrophy and hair separates from the follicle and falls out. This is the catagen or transitional phase. In the resting or telogen phase, the follicles are inactive and have shrunk to about half their normal size. After a relatively short rest period, they regenerate themselves and again begin producing hair. Hair growth cycles

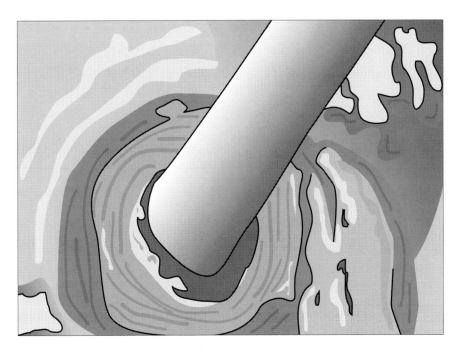

Figure 5-1
Microscopic view of hair follicle

are staggered among the follicles. Not all of the follicles produce hair at the same time.

Each follicle follows its own cycle. At any given time, 85% of the follicles are in the anagen phase. Two percent are in the catagen phase and 13% are in the telogen phase. In people with normally functioning hair follicles, the anagen phase can last up to 5 years, the catagen phase up to 3 weeks, and the telogen phase up to 12 weeks.

Some hair shedding is a normal part of the telogen phase. However, male pattern baldness is a genetic trait. The most common form is bitemporal hair loss and is shared equally by black and white men. Crown pattern baldness, which occurs at the scalp vertex is less common and occurs later in blacks. Because hair length and growth are determined at birth, products promoted to grow hair do not really grow new hair as much as they promote better hair care, which in turn, extends the growth cycle to its maximum length.

The scalp is an area of the skin and its structure is the same as skin anywhere else on the body. The scalp, however, is an area of high activity and is highly complex. Hair-producing cells in the follicles divide more rapidly than any other cells in the body except for those in the bone marrow. The scalp in black skin is usually drier because of the curved hair follicles, which prevent the oils from passing freely through them.

The scalp is often exposed to harmful depredations. Overly aggressive daily grooming of the hair is a major cause of scalp irritation. The idea of brushing the hair vigorously 100 strokes per day is a harmful myth that can easily lead to serious hair damage. Some products commonly used in the care of black hair can irritate the scalp and create dryness, too. No-lye relaxers can be especially drying to the scalp because of the longer processing time they require.

Brushing the hair 100 strokes daily is actually very harmful!

Dandruff is a condition caused by an accelerated turnover of skin cells on the scalp and consequent flaking off in clumps. Some medical conditions, certain hair care products, and inherent scalp dryness can all cause dandruff.

Seborrheac dermatitis and psoriasis can be present on the scalp, just as they can be present on any other area of the skin. All of these conditions can be present in black skin. Contact dermatitis, the dryness, itching, flaking, and pustules, can be caused by hair care products such as relaxers and hot combs. Any of these conditions can lead to temporary or permanent hair loss.

BASIC HAIR STRUCTURE

Black hair and Caucasian hair consist of the same basic structural materials. Both are made from keratin, which is also a basic structural material of skin. Keratin, a protein derived from amino acids, is composed of organic compounds containing carbon, nitrogen, and hydrogen. Keratin also contains sulfur.

Cystine, the sulfur-containing amino acid from which keratin derives, is a major structural component of hair and the one on which relaxers and permanent waves work to alter the shape of the hair.

Black hair generally has a larger diameter and retains less water than white hair. The follicle in black hair is curved and produces hair that is twisted in a spiral. The cross-sectional shape of black hair tends to be flatter, more elliptical than round.

These characteristics—lower water content, curved follicles, and flatter hair shape—may account for the "kinky" hair common to most black people. These same characteristics may also account for difficulty in combing the hair, excessive breakage, and decreasing gloss.

Hair is divided into two basic parts—the shaft and the root (Figure 5-2, next page). The shaft is the part that extends above the skin surface; the root is the part that is below the surface. The bulb is at the lower end of the root, covering the papilla, which nourishes it. Only the root actually grows. The root is living tissue. The shaft, on the other hand, is nonliving matter.

The three horny layers in the hair shaft are the cuticle, the cortex, and the medulla. The outer layer, the cuticle, is transparent. The middle layer, the cortex, contains the pigment that gives the hair its color. Together, these two layers give the hair its strength, flexibility, moisture absorbency, color,

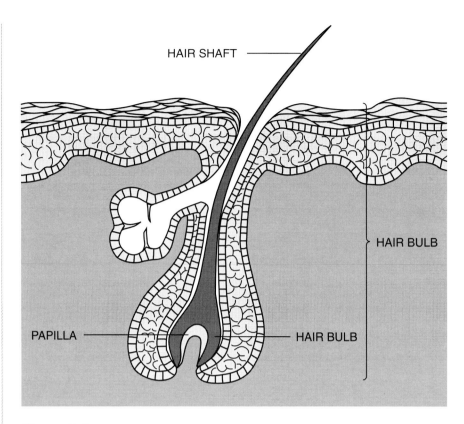

HAIR SHAFT

HAIR BULB

PAPILLA

HAIR BULB

Figure 5-2
Hair structure

and shine. The innermost layer, the medulla, makes up the core of the hair shaft. Its exact functions are not well defined. The hair shaft has no nerve endings, thus, no sensations are felt through the hair, which is why it does not hurt to get a haircut.

The cuticles of black hair tend to be rougher than those in white hair. As a result, black hair cuticles reflect less light, giving a dull appearance to the hair. Since black hair cuticles are less absorbent to moisture, they react differently to chemicals than white hair, and therefore may require special moisturizers and chemical treatments that are longer or different. Black hair cuticles generally have larger melanin granules than those in white hair. This may be the reason black hair lightens in shorter time than white hair.

> Haircuts are not painful because the hair shaft has no nerve endings.

Black hair has a smaller cortex than white hair. This also affects chemical treatments. Timing is especially critical for chemical treatments on black hair, so these services should be performed only by someone highly trained in their use. Once the chemicals pass through the cuticle, they will work quickly on the smaller cortex and alter its structure faster. Black women have a special problem because of this. If the cortex is overprocessed, the hair will become weak, dull, and break off.

The smaller cortex in black hair leads also to a somewhat different sulfur structure and a lower lipid content. The sulfur bonds in black hair are slanted at sharp angles. The bonds are angled in the spiral hair follicle. This accounts for the curly nature of black hair.

The lower lipid content is evident in the inherent dryness common to black hair. Another possible cause of dry hair inherent in blacks is that as hair oils are produced by the sebaceous glands and secreted into the spiral hair follicles, the oils do not always get to the surface to moisturize the hair and scalp.

HAIR ANALYSIS

Just like the skin, hair should be analyzed to determine its type and condition before performing any grooming service or chemical treatment. Hair type is described as straight, wavy or curly, or excessively curly. Each of these types has structural differences. Straight hair is round; wavy hair is oval; curly hair is flat. These are general guidelines, however, and not absolutes. The true variations in hair types are endless because of the possible genetic mix.

The esthetician must understand the differences in density, structure, content and attainable length in black, Asian, and white clients.

Black and Asian hair types are different from white hair types. These differences are described in terms of density, structure, content, and attainable length, all of which are critical factors in formulating hair care products and performing hair services.

Black hair tends to be shorter in length, with an elliptical, almost kidney-shaped form. It requires less force to remove from the scalp and has a higher amino acid content than either white or Asian hair types. Black hair has a greater density than white hair but a lower density than Asian hair.

Black hair services commonly include exposing the hair to high temperatures, as in hot combing, and exposing it to harsh chemicals, as with relaxing, waving, and coloring. This can lead to hair dryness and breakage. In addition, combing black hair puts tremendous mechanical tension on the hair, causing even more dryness and breakage.

Asian hair is normally straight. It grows to greater lengths and has a higher density than either black or white hair. Asian hair requires a greater force than is required with either black or white hair to pull it from the scalp. It is round in shape and has a comparatively low amino acid content. Services for Asian hair are similar to those for white hair. Permanent wave and color treatments can leave Asian hair with a dull and rough appearance.

Hair *texture* is determined by the size of the individual strands. The diameter of the hair is based on the size of the cuticle and the cortex. Coarse hair tends to be larger in diameter than fine hair. This is probably because of the larger cuticle common to coarse and curly black hair.

Hair texture can be divided into seven categories, based on strand diameter: very fine, fine, medium fine, medium, medium coarse, coarse, and very coarse. However, any given strand can have a combination of these textures throughout its length.

Hair Condition

Hair condition is determined by a strand test. One aspect is its *porosity,* or ability to absorb moisture. The more porous the hair, the faster it will absorb moisture. Black hair is less porous than white hair; consequently, chemical treatments require longer times to work.

The second aspect determining hair condition is *elasticity.* Elasticity is the ability of the hair to bend and stretch without breaking off. Hair with good elasticity can tolerate chemical treatments better.

The third and final aspect of hair condition is *density.* Hair density is determined by the number of hairs per square inch. Thick hair will have more hair per square inch than thin hair. Hair density is not related to hair texture. Fine hair can have a high density, just as coarse hair can have a low density.

Hair analysis is the first critical step in the proper care and treatment of the hair. It is important for the stylist and the consumer to realize that different types of hair can differ in response to chemical services.

BLACK HAIR CARE

Shampooing

Black hair tends to be naturally curly, somewhat dry and dull, and breaks easily. Because frequent shampooing can further dry the hair and accelerate breakage, black hair is generally shampooed less frequently (once or twice a week) than white hair. White hair, on the other hand, tends to be oily and requires frequent shampooing to prevent oil buildup and limp hair (Figure 5-3).

Once black hair is wet, it spontaneously starts to curl. This makes styling very difficult. Black hair is not cut while wet because it would be dramatically shorter after it dries. Also, black hair usually requires a spe-

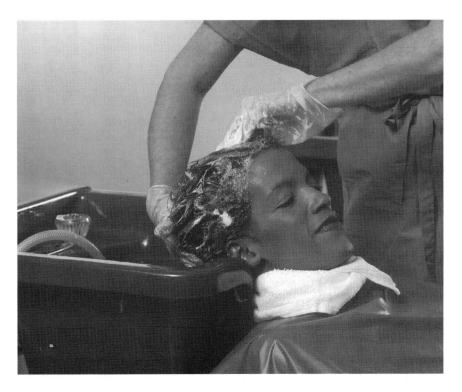

Figure 5-3
Shampooing

cial heating or chemical treatment to style (straighten) the hair. This is most commonly done in a salon. Black women tend to visit their salons at least two to three times a month.

Shampooing is designed to clean the scalp and hair. Because of its characteristics, serious consideration must be given to choosing a shampoo for black hair; the choice should be based on the hair type and condition. The stylist should also be aware of the client's hair history, home hair care regimen, and personal preferences.

Shampoos for black hair most often will need to contain mild detergent cleaners and moderate to heavy conditioners, and have a balanced pH.

Most medicated or dandruff-control shampoos contain ingredients such as tar derivatives, sulfur, selenium sulfide, zinc pyrithione, and salicylic acid. They are formulated to work on the scalp to remove dead skin cells and to slow down cell turnover rate. They can be extremely drying to the hair and scalp. Therefore, these shampoos are seldom effective on black hair, nor are they recommended because they can further dry black hair and scalp.

Medicated and dandruff-control shampoos are not recommended for black hair because they can be extremely drying to the hair and scalp.

To shampoo properly, first wet the hair thoroughly with warm water, then pour a small amount (about the size of a silver dollar) of shampoo into the palm of the hand. Gently massage the shampoo into the scalp starting at the sides of the head near the ears. Gently massage in a back and forth motion from the front hair line to the nape of the neck. Rinse the shampoo from the hair thoroughly with lots of warm water. Repeat the process if necessary. Always make sure to rinse the hair until it is completely free of residual shampoo.

Hair Conditioners

After shampooing, hair has a positive charge, which repels each strand and prevents the hair from lying down, making it more difficult to manage. Hair conditioners are designed to provide moisture, shine, and manageability to hair. They accomplish this by giving the cuticle a neutral charge, thus restoring it to a smooth state and decreasing the ability of the hair to stick together. When it has a neutral charge, black hair becomes easier to comb and brush.

Conditioners also normalize cuticles by alleviating defects in the cuticles to give hair a shine and decrease tangling. Normalized cuticles reflect light more, giving hair a shine. Because strands do not stick together, tangling is decreased and overall manageability is increased. Black hair requires the applications of conditioners after each shampooing.

Three types of conditioners are used with black hair—instant, deep penetrating, and hot oil. *Instant conditioners* are the products used commonly after shampooing in the home and in the salon. They require no mixing and are used right from the bottle. These conditioners are available in various formulations based on hair type and condition. Conditioners formulated with quaternary ammonium compounds work best with black hair. They are excellent for moisturizing the hair, neutralizing the charge on hair to prevent tangling, and providing good shine after smoothing cuticles.

Deep penetrating conditioners are designed for use on dry and damaged hair. They are a concentrated form of instant conditioners and are usually found in a cream form that requires activation by the application of heat, as with a hair dryer or a warm towel. The heat is usually applied for 20 to 30 minutes to allow the hair shaft to swell, increasing porosity and absorption of conditioners that seal and repair damaged cuticles.

Hot oil conditioners are designed to treat extra dry and damaged hair. This treatment is somewhat of a misnomer in that the oils only coat the hair. The actual work is done by proteins and polymers. Hot oil treatments require heating the oil and applying it to the hair, then covering the hair with a plastic cap for the recommended period of time. The treatment provides a shine to the hair and helps repair damaged cuticles.

The hair shaft consists of dead keratin, just like the stratum corneum layer of the skin. The only conditioning treatment that will work is one that coats the hair shaft. Proper conditioning of black hair makes it more manageable, easier to comb and brush; it gives hair a shine and makes it less likely to break. Because the ends are the oldest part of the hair as well as its driest part, apply the conditioners specifically to the end tips and comb thoroughly to provide even distribution of conditioner to the entire hair shaft from the top of the scalp to the end of each hair. Leave the conditioner on for the entire time stated in the manufacturer's instructions.

Chemical Treatments for Black Hair

Most of the hair styles worn by black women today require that she change her hair from its natural curly state to a straight, shiny appearance. This currently fashionable look is accomplished by applying and combing a cream-based product that is highly alkaline through the hair. It is estimated that almost 80% of black women in the United States routinely relax their hair.

Hair relaxers are oil-in-water creams that produce chemical, thermal, and mechanical reactions to the hair. The high alkalinity causes the hair structure to become relaxed and the curly hair becomes straight. Some black women report increased hair growth after using hair relaxers. This is most likely due to decreased breakage of the hair because the now straightened hair undergoes less friction during combing.

Conditioners must be used after the relaxing process because the relaxer can dry and dehydrate the hair, which can also lead to hair loss or damage. Conditioners restore lost moisture and bring the cuticle back to its normal state.

Relaxers are divided into two groups—lye based and no-lye based. *Lye-based relaxers* are usually formulated with sodium hydroxide or potassium hydroxide, both of which are strong bases. They work by converting the double-bonded cystine that makes up curly hair into single-bonded cystine, which allows the curly hair to relax and straighten. The hair then reforms its double bonds for strength, but now the double-bonded strands are straight instead of curved.

Relaxing the hair makes it soft and straight. The relaxing process is stopped when the hair is shampooed with an acidic shampoo. These products should only be used by experienced stylists to prevent chemical burns

Because approximately 80% of black women routinely relax their hair, estheticians must be knowledgeable about the products available and used.

of the scalp, which can lead to permanent hair loss and severe hair damage. With a pH between 10 and 14, lye-based relaxers are extremely caustic. These products are usually found in salons but not in retail stores.

No-lye relaxers are combination products that require mixing two chemicals together to start the relaxing process. The two primary ingredients in these products are calcium hydroxide and guanidine carbonate. When mixed together, they undergo a chemical reaction that forms guanidine hydroxide and calcium carbonate. The calcium carbonate is an inert by-product that plays no part in the relaxing process. The guanidine hydroxide, however, is strongly alkaline and, like the lye-based relaxers, does the actual work.

There is a misconception that no-lye relaxers are harmless and will not damage the hair. This is not true! Both types of relaxers rely on the action of strongly alkaline solutions and the pH of both is about the same. Both must be handled with care by experienced stylists.

Although lye-based relaxers do not require premixing of ingredients; they are more concentrated and relax the hair faster; they need a shorter contact time on the hair and scalp. Thus, they have a higher potential for scalp irritation than no-lye relaxers. In comparison, no-lye relaxers require premixing of ingredients. Their main advantage is the reduced potential for scalp irritation. These products require a longer contact time than the lye-based relaxers and can leave the hair more dry. In addition, the calcium salt can deposit a residue on the hair, making it look dull and stiff.

Relaxers, regardless of kind, are available in three strengths for use on different hair types. The strength of a relaxer is directly related to its hydroxide concentration. Mild strength relaxers have a hydroxide concentration of 1.85 to 2.00. This strength is recommended for fine hair and for porous, damaged hair. With these hair types, the processing time is shorter, which reduces the possibility of further damage to the hair or scalp.

Normal strength relaxers have a hydroxide concentration of 2.06 to 2.20. This strength is recommended for normal hair, coarse hair, and hair with a high density. These hair types require longer contact times, which can potentially cause damage to the hair and scalp. It is important to comb the relaxer into the hair thoroughly to ensure good distribution and even penetration to each hair shaft.

Resistant strength relaxers have a hydroxide concentration of 2.25 to 2.40. This strength is recommended for resistant hair that is tightly woven. This is a potentially dangerous concentration for the scalp and the hair. Because this type of hair usually has a high sulfur concentration and requires increased contact times to allow the relaxer to penetrate the hair shaft, there is an increased risk of damage to the hair or irritation to the scalp.

HAIRCOLORING

Hair, as well as skin, can change its color with age. Gray hair usually appears in whites in their 30s and in blacks in their 40s. Coloring the hair can prolong a youthful appearance as well as giving the hair more depth, volume, silkiness, and contrast. Haircoloring can be used for more than covering gray and restoring the hair's natural color, however. It can also be used to change the hair's natural color. This requires somewhat more care with black hair than with white hair. The haircolor chosen should complement the person's natural skin tones and eye coloration.

Haircoloring can be used to color gray hair, restore the hair's natural color, or change the hair's natural color.

Natural hair color is determined by melanin granules in the cuticle and cortex of the hair strand. The hair's natural color can be changed by artificial means, either by adding color to the natural pigment or by lightening the natural pigment. When lightened, hair goes through seven levels of color change—black, brown, red, red-gold, gold, yellow, and pale yellow.

The natural color of black hair ranges from dark brown with reddish overtones to jet black. Covering gray and restoring its natural color can be accomplished with single-process coloring or, in some cases, with rinses. Making the hair darker than its natural color can also be accomplished with single-process coloring. However, making the hair color significantly lighter than its natural color will almost always require a double-process coloring in which the hair is first stripped of its natural color and then the new tint is applied.

For the most part, the same products and haircoloring techniques used on white hair can be used on black hair, with allowances for time and application procedures for the increased coarseness and porosity of black hair. Coloring black hair is an area that should only be done by trained professionals who are experienced in coloring black hair. Relaxed hair should not be colored permanently. The stress of so much chemical treatment will almost assuredly cause hair breakage and damage. Rinses, however, may be used. As with any chemical service, a patch test and hair analysis should be completed before coloring a person's hair.

There are four categories of artificial haircoloring: gradual, temporary, semipermanent, and permanent.

Gradual Haircoloring

Gradual haircoloring is achieved by the daily application of a product containing a metallic dye that gradually darkens the hair over a 2- to 3-week time span. Most of these products are over-the-counter items sold at retail outlets. The metallic dyes most often used are compounds of lead and silver. Over time, these products can cause the hair to appear dull. They may also weaken the hair and lead to hair breakage. The products are safe to the hair, however, because they do not penetrate the cuticle. They only coat the hair shaft.

Previous use of metallic dye products can alter the results of any chemical service. As a result, stylists should know whether or not a client has used these products before beginning any other type of chemical service.

Temporary Haircoloring

Temporary haircoloring lasts from shampoo to shampoo and is accomplished with rinses that must be reapplied frequently. The rinses, which are acid-based dyes, only improve the existing color. Like the metallic dyes,

> Even with a patch test and hair analysis, coloring of black hair should be done only by experienced personnel.

rinses coat the cuticle without penetrating into the hair shaft. As a result, they are not likely to damage the hair.

When using a rinse to add color to the cuticle of black hair, the color service should be planned to coincide with a relaxer service. This will enhance and prolong the hair color.

Semipermanent Haircoloring

As the name of the category implies, semipermanent haircoloring lasts longer than shampoo to shampoo but does not permanently change the hair color. Hair colored by this method will hold color through four to six shampoo cycles.

Semipermanent haircoloring is achieved with synthetic or natural dyes that produce a tone-on-tone color change. They do not produce dramatic color changes. Synthetic dyes are coal tar derivatives that must be approved by the Food and Drug Administration for cosmetic use.

Natural dyes are derived from vegetable matter and are the oldest type of hair colorants known. The most common natural dye is henna, which comes from the henna plant. The form most used today is compound henna, in which metallic dyes are added to the henna to give a wider range of colors. Compound henna is safer to use than natural henna, which can cause dryness, stiffness, and hair breakage. Natural henna does have a very low allergic profile, however.

Semipermanent haircolorants, whether natural or synthetic, cannot lighten darker hair. They can only make hair darker. They can darken lighter hair up to three shades. These products penetrate the cuticle and reach the cortex, although they do this without using ammonia and hydrogen peroxide. Body temperature and dryer heat decrease reaction time for the products to work and increase the level of penetration of the dye to the cortex.

Permanent Haircoloring

Permanent haircoloring changes the chemical structure of the hair and, as a result, lasts until the hair grows out enough to require a touch-up. This could be anywhere from 4 to 6 weeks after the initial coloring takes place.

The natural color of the person's hair can be lightened or darkened, depending on the new color desired.

Permanent haircoloring is the most common type of hair coloring in current use. Formulations are available for home use as well as for professional salon use. The chemistry is basically the same regardless of the formulation, although those products designed for professional salon use are typically stronger and allow more dramatic changes in hair color.

In general, permanent haircoloring products consist of hydrogen peroxide, ammonia, and a colorant. The formulation works by penetrating the hair shaft into the cortex. To lighten the hair and prepare it to accept the colorant, the melanin granules that give the hair its natural color have to be destroyed by a chemical reaction known as oxidation. Hydrogen peroxide is the oxidizing agent that accomplishes this step. The ammonia is an activating agent for the peroxide. The colorant provides the color.

A number of different colorants are used for permanent haircoloring. The most commonly used are aniline derivative tints, which have some oxidizing action of their own. These colorants are known to cause allergic reactions or contact dermatitis in a certain percentage of the population. When using any of these products, it is necessary to conduct a patch test first.

Always **conduct a patch test before applying permanent haircoloring.**

To conduct a patch test, mix a small amount of the product as it would be used normally, then apply a small amount of it to the back of the ear area and leave on for 24 hours. If the test is negative, that is, there is no reaction, the product may be used. If the test is positive, that is, there is redness, swelling, itching, blistering, or pain, the product should not be used.

Hair damage is quite common with permanent haircoloring. The hair can become dull and lifeless as well as discolored, and it can weaken and break. Special conditioning steps may be prudent to maintain the health of the hair. Hair relaxing or permanent wave treatments should not be given within 10 days of coloring the hair and should be conducted only by a trained and experienced professional.

Permanent haircoloring treatments can be either single process or double process. Both processes can lighten or darken the hair color. Most home coloring formulations are single process. Professional treatments can use either.

In single-process coloring, the colorant is mixed with the peroxide. The mixture is applied as a single step. The peroxide lifts the color and prepares the cortex for the colorant. The colorant finishes the work.

In double-process coloring, two steps are used. First, hydrogen peroxide is used to remove the existing color. Second, the colorant is used to provide the new color. The double-process treatment results in the most dramatic color changes.

Because of its thicker cuticle, virgin black hair has a low porosity and is more resistant to hair coloring than Caucasian hair. However, the various chemical treatments that black hair requires can increase the porosity, making black hair more receptive to coloring. The cortex in black hair is thinner than in Caucasian hair. As a result, once the color formulation gets past the cuticle, the time required for the service is reduced.

Lightening black hair requires a higher concentration of hydrogen peroxide than is needed to lighten Caucasian hair. Whereas 20 volume hydrogen peroxide is normal for use on Caucasian hair, for black hair, the concentration may reach 25 to 30 volume. Black hair should never be lightened beyond the red-gold level because that will almost always cause damage. Black hair that has been chemically treated with perms or relaxers should not be lightened.

PERMANENT WAVING

Permanent waving chemically alters the disulfide bond of the hair, changing its elasticity and allowing it to be formed to a different shape. This usually involves making the hair more curly.

Products for permanent waving are available in different types. As with hair colorants, these products are available in home use formulations and professional use formulations. The ingredients for both types are similar, but those for home use have a lower pH, usually in the 6 to 8 range, and are designed to give looser curls that will last for a shorter duration.

The higher the pH of an alkaline permanent, the tighter and more long-lasting the curls will be. Professional grade perms have a pH in the 9 to 10 range. These products have a shorter processing time than the less alkaline perms, but can be damaging to the hair. They can cause dryness and frizziness.

Typical active ingredients in permanent wave lotions are ammonium thioglycolate or calcium thioglycolate, with ammonium bicarbonate used as a buffer. These ingredients can cause allergic reactions or contact dermatitis, so a patch test should be conducted before using them.

In the standard procedure for giving a permanent, the hair is shampooed. The damp hair is rolled on rollers that approximate the desired curl size. End papers are used to prevent frizzy ends. The wave lotion is then applied. The lotion breaks the disulfide bond. After the time specified by the manufacturer of the product, the wave lotion is neutralized to an acid pH with an oxidizing agent. This process restores the disulfide bonds, fixing the hair in the new position determined by the rollers. The permanent wave will last for 4 to 6 months.

The permanent wave process may be either cold or hot. In the cold process, the buffered thioglycolic acid wave lotion is applied and the hair is covered with a plastic cap. The body's natural heat supplies the warmth needed for the process. The hot process is similar, except that a dryer is used to supply the heat. Heat processing is more likely to cause scalp irritation and should be used with caution.

BRAIDING AND HAIR WEAVING

Braiding and hair weaving are currently popular fashions, particularly among black women. Both are similar, in that they are made by interweaving strands of hair. Braiding, however, is done solely with the person's natural hair. Hair weaving, on the other hand, uses human hair that has been matched to the person's natural hair for color and texture. This supplemental hair, as it were, is woven into braids intertwined with the natural hair.

These styles are accomplished by mechanical actions, with no chemicals used, so there is no concern about chemical irritation. However, the tight braids currently in vogue can lead to some hair damage. It takes a considerable amount of time to have such braiding or weaving done. In some cases, sessions in the salon can take up to 8 hours. Once done, the braids are kept in for weeks. With very tight braids, it is difficult to properly clean the scalp and hair because water and shampoos cannot penetrate into the braids. This can create problems with skin irritation and infection. To overcome this, some women wash their braided hair with water-pics designed for dental use.

> The currently fashionable tight braids may cause some hair damage.

In addition, tight braiding can cause breakage and hair loss due to a condition known as traction alopeceia, in which the hair is almost literally pulled out of its roots.

HAIR LOSS

Hair loss is defined as the obvious loss of large amounts of scalp hair or body hair or as the loss of the quality of scalp hair, for example, diminishment of diameter, length, and density.

Hair loss can be caused by a number of conditions, some of which can affect only the hair, or only the scalp, or a combination of both. Some common causes of hair loss include poor diet, rapid weight loss, drugs, family history (i.e., genetic predisposition), recent illnesses, improper hair care, aging, and hormone imbalances. Hair can also be lost in a period starting 2 to 3 months after pregnancy and can last for up to 9 months. Hair loss as a result of excessive breakage is usually caused by improper hair care.

Androgenic Alopeceia

The most common form of hair loss in women and men is androgenic alopeceia. Thirty percent of Caucasian women are affected with this condition before the onset of menopause. Androgenic alopeceia is sometimes reversible with medical treatment, but the results of treatment are unpredictable. Results depend on individual sensitivity to medical treatment.

This form of alopeceia is believed to be caused by higher than normal levels of circulating androgens that stimulate genetically sensitive hair follicles and shorten the anagen phase of the hair growth cycle. At the same time, there is an increased shedding of hair from follicles in the telogen phase.

Pattern Baldness

Male pattern baldness occurs in the frontotemporal regions and at the vertex. Female pattern baldness is more diffuse although hair is not usually lost on the frontal hair line. Either pattern can be seen in women of any age.

Traumatic Alopeceia

Traumatic alopeceia is common in blacks and is caused by chemical and mechanical abuse of the hair and scalp. Chemical treatments can cause extreme breakage of the hair and lead to this type of alopeceia. Tightly braiding the hair can also cause severe irritation to the scalp, which releases the hair from the follicle and causes the condition. Traumatic alopeceia is usually reversible. The condition is best treated with better hair care.

Alopeceia Areata

Alopeceia areata is sometimes a reversible form of hair loss that features well-circumscribed, nonscarring patches of baldness. This is a common condition among almost all age groups beyond the teen years. There is a considerable variation in the rate and pattern of hair loss and regrowth. Most sufferers of this condition are in good general health, although a number of diseases have also been associated with the onset of alopeceia areata. These include asthma, atopic dermatitis, diabetes, thyroid disease, ulcerative colitis, and vitiligo.

The many types of hair loss can have an equal number of causes.

Ten percent of people with alopeceia areata also undergo changes in the nails. These changes include pitting, longitudinal ridging, thickening, brittleness, and onchylysis. Twenty-five percent of people have a family history of the condition.

In 90% of the cases, the condition follows a pattern in which there is patchy hair loss for a 3- to 6-month period. This is followed by a 3- to 6-

month period of stability, after which there is a 3- to 6-month period of gradual regrowth. Recurrence of the condition is common, although complete permanent hair loss is rare.

There is no consistent effective treatment for alopeceia areata. The course of treatment is variable between regrowth and remission stages. Currently available treatments include topical and injectable steroids, minoxidil, psoralen plus ultraviolet A (PUVA), and perhaps most important, psychological support from family and friends.

Telogen Effluvium

Telogen effluvium is an abrupt form of hair loss in which half or less of the scalp hair is lost because of a severe assault on the body's metabolism. The stimulus for the condition causes a large number of anagen hairs to convert to telogen hairs with subsequent shedding. The condition normally appears 1 to 4 months after the metabolic event. Some metabolic assaults that can lead to telogen effluvium include childbirth, chronic illness, rapid weight change, high fever, hypothyroidism, psychological stress, surgery, and systemic infection. No treatment is necessary for this condition because it is inherently self-limiting. Hair regrowth is almost always complete within 6 months to a year.

Anagen Effluvium

Anagen effluvium is also associated with metabolic assault. In this condition, there is a rapid and incomplete conversion of anagen hair to telogen hair leading to the diffuse shedding of 85% to 90% of the scalp hair. This condition is similar to telogen effluvium but occurs to a greater degree. Regrowth is common when the underlying metabolic condition is corrected.

Drug-Induced Alopeceia

In drug-induced alopeceia, drugs taken or chemicals used increase the number of hairs in the telogen phase, which leads to telogen effluvium. It can also be caused when the drugs or chemicals produce a dermatologic condition that features alopeceia as a symptom. A wide variety of drugs can cause drug-induced alopeceia, including amphetamines, haloperidol, heparin, indomethacin, isotretinoin, lithium, propranol, and many others. Treatment for the condition consists of controlling or eliminating the offending drug.

Scarring Alopeceia

In scarring alopeceia, the capacity of the follicle to function is lost because of trauma or disease. The condition is irreversible. The most common disease that causes scarring alopeceia is discoid lupus erythematosus (DLE). DLE lesions can be seen in people with systemic disease involvement, although they are commonly seen alone as well. In black women, the lesions are most common in areas of the skin exposed to the sun.

The scarring shows as a hypopigmented, atrophic plaque with teleangectasia on the face, neck, ears, and scalp. UV light makes the lesions worse, so sun protection is mandatory. The cause of DLE is unknown. Treatment is more effective on early lesions. The condition is treated with anti-inflammatory steroids.

Hair loss is a common complaint. Professional beauty care providers will often see clients who are suffering from hair loss to some degree. Although it is important the provider recognize some of the symptoms, in almost all cases, he or she should refer the client to a physician for diagnosis and treatment. These are, for the most part, medical conditions that require the services of a trained, licensed physician.

NAILS AND THEIR CARE

In today's beauty business climate, it is just as important to know and understand care and treatment of finger and toenails as it is hair and skin. The nails are an important part of a person's appearance. Nail care services are desired by both men and women. Most people view the service as a well-deserved investment in themselves.

Nail care is a vital part of the salon's service!

Counting nail services and retail sales of products, the nail business is currently a $40 billion market. Salon owners are realizing the added respect and revenue nail services can bring to their businesses. Nail services require more frequent follow-up than any other service provided by a salon. The average beauty conscious nail client requires an appointment every 2 weeks.

In addition to manicures, currently popular nail services include fills, artificial nail application, and nail art. Nor are the feet being overlooked. Pedicures have become increasingly popular. Clients are constantly looking for products and services that will enhance the appearance of their hands and nails.

Today's nail care products are the result of modern technology and the desire for more natural-looking nails. Early nail enhancement products tended to prevent the nail from breathing and trapped moisture. This led to infections and other nail problems. Newer products let the nail respire and are safer to use.

The nails are hard, highly keratinized structures located at the ends of the fingers and toes. Growing outward from the malpighian layer of the epidermis, these translucent, cornified plates serve to protect the sensitive ends of the digits.

The current focus is on the care of the natural nail, as the emphasis moves to preserving and protecting the integrity of the natural nail plate. Nail services should avoid rough handling, mechanical operations, or harsh chemicals that could damage the nail plate. Consultation should be given before any service is started. Information gathered by the nail technician during the consultation should include the client's lifestyle, level of activity, fashion preferences, along with the shape and condition of the natural nails.

Artificial Nails

Artificial nails can be used to enhance nail beauty. Artificial nails can hold polish much longer and provide a smoother surface. Artificial nails come in many different types based on shape, length, and thickness.

Preformed nails are made of a light plastic that is preformed to fit many nail sizes. They are adhered to the natural nail with glue. This type of artificial nail is generally of poor quality and does not offer much endurance.

Acrylic nails are made from a fine mesh fabric stiffened with an acrylic resin to create a natural looking nail cover. The nails are actually a sculptured mold of the mesh/polymer combination. The nails are attached with chemical adhesives and enhance nail length and appearance. This type of artificial nail is generally of high quality and is long lasting. However, the acrylic polymers or the adhesives can cause allergic reactions.

Sculptured nails are formed by applying an acrylic polymer to the natural nail, slowly and gently building it up to the desired length and shape. The polymer is cured, leaving a perfectly shaped nail that has a good appearance and lasts a long time. As the natural nail grows, however, the sculptured nail moves away from the cuticle and leaves a space that must be filled in with new polymer. This must be done every 2 to 3 weeks. These artificial nails can also damage the nail plate.

Nail Structure and Growth

The *nail plate* is made of keratin, the same material that makes up the hair shafts and the stratum corneum layer of the epidermis. The plate, which is essentially dead matter, contains no blood vessels, nerves, or fat cells. This is the part of the nail structure on which nail technicians do their cutting, trimming, polishing, and coloring. It is also where artificial nails are attached.

The nail plate lies on the *nail bed,* an area of modified dermal tissue that contains a blood supply. The back edge of the nail plate is covered by a bit of skin, known as the *cuticle.* The crescent-shaped area under the cuticle is called the *lunula.*

The nails begin to grow 10 weeks after conception while the fetus is in the embryonic stage. They continue to grow until death. Growth begins in the nail matrix. The end result is the nail plate. On average, fingernails grow at a rate of 3 mm per month; toenails grow about 1.5 mm per month. Faster nail growth is common during pregnancy, during menstruation, and dur-

Nails grow from the fetal embryonic stage 10 weeks after conception until the person dies.

ing the summer season. People between the ages of 20 and 40 have the fastest nail growth. Nail growth is greater on the person's dominant hand. The nail on the middle finger grows faster than on the other fingers. Nail growth slows with age or during illness. A finger nail broken off at the root will take 3 to 6 months to grow to normal length.

A number of factors and conditions promote nail growth. The first, and most important, is good, consistent nail care. Nails should be manicured once a month. The use of acetone and formaldehyde-based polish removers should be limited. The nails and the area around the nails should be conditioned daily.

Although some people may find extra long fingernails attractive, some dangers are involved. Long fingernails are more subject to damage. They are harder to keep clean and can harbor infectious agents. Long nails can make relatively easy chores more difficult. For most effective nail care, the nails should be kept short.

Nail Health

Although the actual nail plate is translucent white, when pressed against the nail bed it appears pink, at least if it is healthy. Like the skin and hair, nails can also provide a window to someone's health. Several medical conditions can be spotted by examining the nails carefully while preparing them for grooming. For example, if the nail beds are very pale, the client may have an iron deficiency. Similarly, yellow nails may indicate lung disease, diabetes, or nail fungus.

The health of the nails may provide a clue to a person's overall health status.

Physical Defects. Grooves may develop in the nails as the result of alterations in the maturity of the nail cells. Inflammation and trauma at or around the cuticle can lead to nail grooves. Nail discoloration can result from infection, trauma, and systemic conditions or from nail care products that deposit pigment in the nail.

White spots on the nails have been associated with many myths about love life, inheritance, personal integrity, and so on. However, such white spots are a result of minor trauma to the growth area at or around the cuticle.

Weak, brittle nails are usually the result of overexposure to harsh, drying nail care products and detergent cleaners.

Nail separation is the detachment of the nail plate from the nail bed and is usually a result of trauma, infection, allergy to nail products, or over-aggressive cleaning under the nail. Once the nail is detached it cannot be reattached. A new nail must form and this can take from 3 to 6 months.

Infections. Cuticle (eponychium) infections appear as dryness, redness, swelling, and pain around the cuticle. These can occur as a result of over-aggressive manicures, picking and biting the cuticle, chemical irritation, excessive exposure to water, and injury or disease.

Onychomycosis is a fungal infection of the finger and toenails. Nail fungi are very common. The fungi live under the nail plate where they grow in a safe, protected environment. This makes nail fungus infections hard to treat. Infected nails can appear yellow, white, dark, or opaque in color. In toenails, the texture becomes thick and brittle. Long-standing infections can cause the nail plate to become twisted and distorted. Usually, more than one nail is involved in the fungus infection.

Nail fungus infection is acquired in many ways, usually from common, everyday objects like towels, clothing, furniture, at the gym, in the garden, and so on. Fungi thrive in warm, dark, moist places. When the hands or feet are in those same environments, the nails can become infected.

A common myth is that fungal infections result from a lack of cleanliness. This is most assuredly not true! Most nail infections start as the result of a simple injury, such as trimming the nail too close, wearing tight or poorly ventilated shoes, or dropping something on the foot. Any of these can create an environment for the fungus.

Most nail fungal infections are not painful although there can be some discomfort. The greatest effect of nail fungal infections is to the emotional health of the person affected. This is a result of the unsightly appearance of the infected nails. Covering nail fungi

Nail fungal infections do not arise from a lack of cleanliness. Most develop after a simple injury.

will not make them go away. In fact, the infection may progress or develop a secondary bacterial infection, which can be painful.

Bacterial infections of the nails are usually secondary infections resulting from fungal infections or trauma. These infections appear as greenish brown colorations of the nail plate.

Most nail infections require treatment with oral medications. Technological advances in medicine have helped considerably. In the past, treatments for fingernail infections could last from 3 to 6 months and for toenail infections, from 9 months to a year. Taking prescribed medication for these lengths of time increased the chances for systemic side effects, such as kidney or liver problems. However, new medications have reduced the times to 4 to 6 weeks for fingernail infections and 3 months for toenail infections. This has greatly reduced the risk of harmful side effects.

As with many skin and hair conditions, these nail conditions should be treated by a medical doctor. The cosmetologist should refer the client to a physician.

Chapter 6

Makeup for Black Skin

T*he proper use of makeup* is an important aspect of skin and beauty care. In many ways, it can be considered a continuation of the process that began with cleansing and conditioning the skin. Once the skin's functions have been normalized, the face is ready for the application of those cosmetic products that further enhance its appearance.

There are many different types of makeup products, each designed to meet certain requirements in the process of beautifying the face. These include foundation, powder, mascara, blush, lipstick, and a host of other products and accessories. As with any product, however, makeup must be used properly to get the maximum effect possible. Like skin care formulations, makeup products should be chosen to match the person's skin type.

Regardless of the type of makeup, the face must be cleansed thoroughly before application. This includes the use of cleanser, toner, and moisturizer, as described earlier. Only on a clean face can the various makeup products provide and maintain a freshly made up look.

Makeup must be applied only to a clean face—cleansed, toned, and moisturized.

MAKEUP AND COLOR

Color is an important consideration in makeup application. The proper choice of makeup colors, and the color temperature of the light in which the makeup is viewed, will greatly affect the person's look.

Color has two dimensions—the physical and the psychological. The physical dimension of color involves light, shadow, hue, value, intensity, and temperature. Different light sources have different color casts, depending on the color temperature of the source. Incandescent lamps, for example, tend toward the red end of the spectrum; fluorescent lights tend toward the blue end. Even daylight changes color. Depending on the time of day and weather conditions, it can vary from red to blue. Various shades of makeup colors will look different under different lighting. This is the reason makeup must be tailored to the lighting conditions under which it will appear. For example, makeup for an office environment (bright fluorescent lights) will be different from makeup for an evening on the town (dim incandescent lights).

Colors also have temperature. They can be thought of in terms of warm, neutral, or cool. Colors containing a predominance of red or yellow tend to be warm; those containing a predominance of blue or green tend to be cool. White, gray, and black are neutral.

Colors are described in terms of hue, value, and intensity. *Hue* refers to the color itself (e.g., blue, brown, green, yellow). *Value* refers to lightness or darkness (e.g., light green, dark yellow). Darker values are sometimes called shades; lighter values are sometimes called tints. *Intensity* refers to a color's brightness or dullness. Shiny colors appear more intense than matte finish colors. Thus, a shinier makeup will accentuate features, whereas matte finish makeup will diminish them.

There is also a definite psychology of color, both in how colors are perceived and in the moods they evoke. Color is as much a factor of human perception as it is a physical concept. People see colors differently. A shade of red, for example, will look different to a person with blue eyes than it does to a person with brown eyes. In addition, a given color is seen differently depending on the context in which it is viewed. Thus, a bright red dot on a lighter red field would appear more intense than it actually is. The same bright red dot on a darker red field would appear less intense than it actually is.

Light or bright colors appear to come forward or advance. Dark or dull colors appear to move backward or recede. Thus, the use of lighter shades of makeup can accentuate features; the use of darker shades can diminish them.

The psychological effect of color has long been known. Different colors are associated with different states of emotion. Thus, people are said to be "blue" when they are sad; "green" with envy; "yellow" if cowardly; or see "red" when angry. The colors used in the environment can have subtle effects on mood and behavior. Green, for example, is soothing and tranquil; blue promotes a feeling of spaciousness; yellow is cheerful and stimulating.

The proper choice of colors for cosmetics or for fashions plays a significant role in enhancing skin and hair tones. Although colors can be combined in almost limitless numbers, not all combinations are pleasing. Some combinations are harmonious; others clash.

The goal of makeup application is to achieve proportion and balance in appearance. The two keys to proper makeup application are the facial features and the coloration of the skin. This latter can pose significant problems for black women. It is estimated that black skin has 35 different skin tones, ranging from ebony black to almost white. So it is important that a black woman chooses cosmetic colors that complement and enhance her particular skin tone. This is especially true with foundation.

MAKEUP PROBLEMS ON BLACK SKIN

The major problem for a black-skinned woman is to find a foundation that will give her a blemish-free, even-textured, even-colored, and consistent look on her face with no demarcation line in evidence where the foundation stops.

Achieving an even texture with foundation is not always possible. If a woman has a large number of sebaceous glands, especially in the central area of the face, she will tend to have large pores. As a result, she will probably have oily skin in those areas, with the potential for developing acne and discoloration. The ultimate result may be skin with uneven texture and tone. These conditions may be alleviated with medical treatment involving dermabrasion and deep chemical peels, but the efficacy of these treatments for black skin is debatable.

By the same token, it is difficult to achieve even color with the application of foundation because most black women have combination skin, oily in the "T-zone" and dry in the rest of the face. The skin in the oilier areas tends to be lighter and shinier; the skin in the drier areas tends to be darker and duller. This factor, coupled with the wide range of black skin tones, makes it virtually impossible for a standard, over-the-counter foundation to work satisfactorily.

For most black women, the foundation will have to be custom blended, where several different foundation base colors are mixed to match the individual's face and cover any imperfections. Such blending usually requires the services of an experienced makeup artist who has the experience and the talent to determine the skin's undertone and combine the right amount of each color to achieve the perfect look.

Most black women will need a custom-blended foundation, formulated to fit their particular facial characteristics.

MAKEUP APPLICATION

Foundation

The first step in makeup application is the foundation, which provides the base on which the rest of the makeup rests. The primary functions of the foundation are to even out the skin tone and texture of the face and to provide a surface to which the other products will adhere (Figure 6-1).

Black Skin Care for the Practicing Professional

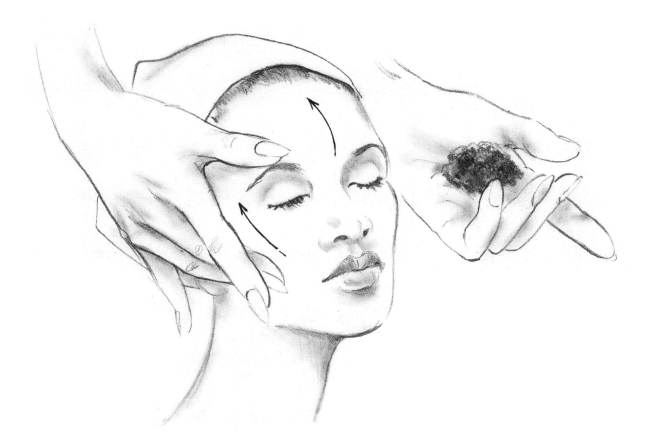

Figure 6-1
Foundation application

Foundations are available in a variety of forms designed to provide any desired degree of convenience and to meet virtually any personal preference. As with skin care products and other makeup items, foundation must match the skin type.

Wet/Dry Powder Foundations. The latest development in foundation chemistry is the wet/dry powder base, a product supplied in the form of a cake and available in formulations for all skin types. The product can be applied wet, with a damp sponge, or it can be applied dry, with a powder puff. Applied wet, the foundation gives a more complete coverage with greater color intensity. Applied dry, it gives a more transparent coverage with a matte finish. This kind of foundation is versatile. It is convenient and provides different types of coverage with one product.

Water-Free Foundations. Water-free foundations are oil-based formulations generally supplied as rather dense creams with a high pigment content. They are formulated for use primarily on dry skin, where they provide a degree of moisturizing. Some of these foundations are marketed as "water-proof" and "nonsmearing" for active lifestyles. These products are slow drying and give a shiny appearance with a "made-up" look. However, they are long lasting and mask imperfections in the skin. Because of their oil content, these foundations are generally not suitable for women with oily skin. They can aggravate acne.

Water-free foundations may not be suitable for use by some black women, especially those with oily skin. Depending on its oiliness, black skin reflects light and gives off a shine. The oil-base foundations can add to this shine, thus perpetuating the myth that black skin is oilier than white skin.

Oil-Free Foundations. Oil-free foundations are water-based formulations containing water as the carrier, mixed with colorant in powder form and emollient esters. These products are generally supplied as liquid suspensions, which must be shaken thoroughly before application. Depending on the emollients used they are available as a light moisturizer or as a drying base. Because they contain no oil, they are suitable for use on oily and problem skin as well as combination skin.

These products are very light and do not cover as well as oil-base or emulsion foundations. They dry to a matte finish that gives the skin a well-balanced look. They dry rapidly, so quick and skilled application may be necessary to prevent uneven coverage.

Oil-free foundations begin to break down in coverage about 2 to 4 hours after application, depending on the environment and on the body's chemistry. Some oil-free foundations turn dark when mixed with the skin's natural oils. As a result, black women may want to purchase these foundations a shade lighter than usual to avoid this.

Emulsion Foundations. Emulsion foundations consist of mixtures of water and oil, held together with emulsifying agents. There are two general types. Water-in-oil (W/O) formulations contain more oil than water; oil-in-water (O/W) formulations contain more water than oil.

The W/O foundations, because of their higher oil content, also act as effective moisturizers for dry skin. They are not recommended for use on oily or combination skin. These products are less oily than oil-base foundations but can still leave the face relatively shiny. (The shine can be minimized with the addition of translucent powder.) These formulations last up to 8 hours. They are slow drying, so they are relatively easy to apply and easier to achieve a more perfect finish. W/O foundations are available in creams, liquids, and soufflés.

The O/W foundations, because of their lower oil content, are recommended for use on oily and combination skin. Their oil content still gives them a moisturizing function. These products are popular because they are light, provide good coverage, and can be applied evenly without leaving a heavy, "made-up" look. They dry relatively rapidly, so quick and skilled application is necessary. These products start to break down in 3 to 5 hours after application, depending on the environment and on the body's chemistry. O/W foundations are available in creams, liquids, soufflés, and aerosols.

Powders

Powders are the next step in proper makeup application. In the past, their primary use was for setting heavy oil-base and W/O emulsion foundations. With the advent of water-base and O/W foundations that give good coverage without an oily, shiny look, as well as improvements in the formulation of the heavier foundations, that use has been largely supplanted. Today, powders are also used to perfect the texture of the skin, but are still used to set foundation and to keep the foundation looking fresher longer. They tend to dull the finish of foundations, providing a matte finish to the makeup.

There are two types of powder makeup products. Loose powders consist of fine-milled pigmented powder with some quantity of dry emollient. They are also available as translucent powders, which provide no coloration of their own. Loose powders are applied gently with a dry puff and provide a silky finish look. These products may be used on any skin type.

Pressed-cake powders, such as found in compacts, are usually made of fine-milled pigmented or translucent powder bound into a cake with oils or other emollients. Those made with oil are recommended for use on dry skin. Those made with non-oily emollients are recommended for use on oily and combination skin.

Specially formulated powder foundations are also available. These products contain absorptive powders with a water-base foundation and are recommended for use with oily or combination skin. They provide good coverage, are less oily, and wear longer.

Blush

Blushers, or rouges, are designed to highlight, maximize, and give a healthy look to the temples and cheek bones. They are available in a variety of colors and can be used either with or without foundation. Blushers are available in powders, creams, gels, and aerosols. As with other makeup products, blushes should be matched to skin type.

Powders and blushes must be matched to skin type—for degree of oiliness and color.

Cream blushers are more difficult to use properly. They are harder to blend and apply than other types of blusher. Powder blushers are the most commonly used type. They are easier to use and can add tremendous color and smooth finish to the cheeks and temples.

Eye Makeup

Eye makeup is the most complex part of makeup application and requires the most skill and knowledge of color chemistry. It is important to use only properly formulated eye makeup that does not contain colorants derived from coal tar, such as those found in some foundations and other cosmetics. Products containing these ingredients should never be used around the eyes.

Sanitation is especially important with eye makeup. The eye area is the most sensitive part of the face and can be more susceptible to infection and irritation than other areas. Eye makeup samples in stores should never be used. Applicators should never be used by more than one person. Eye makeup should be replaced frequently.

Sanitation is critical when applying eye makeup because the eye area is extremely sensitive to damage and infection.

Eyebrow Makeup. The eyebrows are an important facial feature. They help frame the eyes and enhance their appearance. In addition, they can serve as a strong agent of nonverbal communication. Eyebrow makeup is used to improve the appearance of the brows by filling in sparse areas and, after tweezing to reshape the line, to define the eyebrow line. The color of the eyebrow makeup is usually chosen to match the person's hair color (Figure 6-2, next page).

Eyebrow makeup is available in a variety of forms including powders, pencils, crayons, pens, and sealers. Powders can be either water base or oil base. They are messy to use, however, and there is always a possibility of contamination and irritation to the eyes.

Pencils are the most commonly used form of eyebrow makeup. They are easy to control and provide a clean, straight line with less chance of irritation to the eyes. They are usually oil base with the addition of wax to hold the product in its solid form. Crayons are of similar composition, but they provide a less well-defined line and are harder to control. Pens provide a well-defined line and are easy to use. They are liquid rather than solid and are packaged in a device resembling the writing instruments.

Sealers are designed to hold brow hair in place after the line has been defined. They are like miniature liquid versions of hair spray.

Eye Shadow. Eye shadow is designed to accent the eyebrows, eyelids, and the eyes by adding coloration to the skin in the eye area. Eyebrow color is normally chosen to match the person's hair color while the eye shadow color is chosen to complement the person's clothing colors (Figure 6-3, next page).

Figure 6-2
Eyebrow makeup application

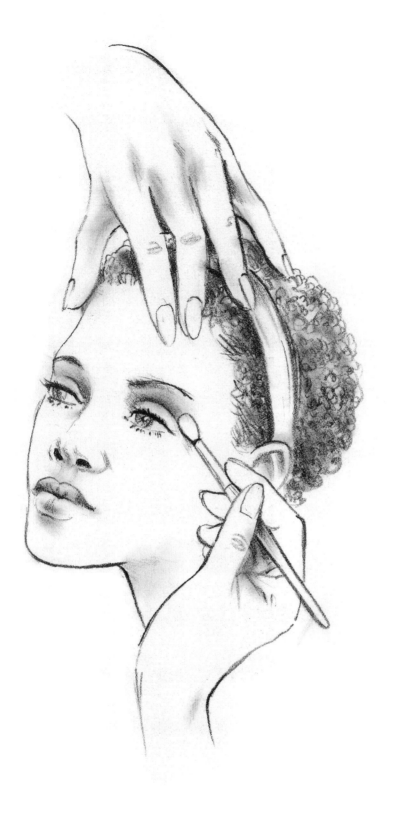

Figure 6-3

Eye shadow application

The skin in the eye area is usually normal to dry on everyone, regardless of skin type on other areas of the face. As a result, skin type is not normally a factor in choosing eye shadow, although eye shadow products for dry and oily skin types are available.

Eye shadows are available in pressed powder, cream, and crayon forms. The pressed powder form is most commonly used because it is easier to apply, provides good control, and has excellent coverage.

Eyeliner. Eyeliner is designed to accent the eye area, usually by adding a dark line of color around the eyes. It may be applied above and below the eyelashes.

Eyeliner products are available in a variety of forms. The choice of eyeliner should be based on the look desired and on personal preference. Pen eyeliners contain liquid makeup in the form of writing pens. They come in water-base and oil-base formulations and are the easiest to apply. They also provide long-lasting color without running. Eyeliner pencils are similar to eyebrow pencils in composition. They are also easy to use, but can be sometimes difficult to remove with some makeup removers.

Powder eyeliners are available, but are harder and messier to use and present more potential for eye irritation. These are usually water-base formulations with emollients added.

Mascara. Mascara is designed to add color to eyelashes and to increase their apparent thickness and length. The mascara color should be chosen to match the person's hair color (See Figure 6-4).

This cosmetic product is available in two basic forms—water-proof and water-resistant. Water-proof mascara provides longer lasting coverage

Because of the risk for infection from contamination, mascara should be replaced every 3 months.

and is more resistant to running. This type is generally applied when the user is engaging in outdoor activities. By contrast, water-resistant mascara lasts for a shorter period of time and breaks down easier when water (e.g., tears and perspiration) form in the eye area. It is more applicable for indoor use.

Figure 6-4
Mascara application

Both are oil-base formulations, although the water-resistant form contains more water. As a result, the water-resistant formulations are easier to apply and remove than the water-proof formulations and are more subject to bacterial contamination. This risk of bacterial contamination is high in either type, however, so mascara should be replaced at 3-month intervals.

Lip Makeup

The lips are very sensitive. The epidermal layer of skin on the lips is very thin, making them prone to dryness, chapping, and discoloration. Women around the world use more lip makeup than any other type of cosmetic product. It adds color to the face and is usually coordinated with clothing colors, blush, and nail polish (Figure 6-5, next page).

Lip makeup is available in a number of forms. Most lip products are water free and contain high levels of oil to help moisturize and protect the lips from sun damage and irritation from constant licking. Lipsticks are the most common form of lip makeup. These are a semisolid blend of oil and wax combined with various pigments to provide the color. They are easy to apply, have good coverage, and are generally long lasting. Application

Figure 6-5

Lip makeup application

Black Skin Care for the Practicing Professional

usually begins at the outer corners of the top lip and works toward the center. This limits the chance of the lipstick making contact with the teeth. The lipstick is applied to the bottom lip by transferring it from the top lip by pressing the bottom lip against the top lip evenly.

Lip crayons are more solid because they contain a higher proportion of wax. They are more difficult to apply than lipsticks but provide excellent coverage and durability. Lip gloss and creams are soft. These products provide moisture and shine to the lips. They are easy to apply but smear easily and lack long-term durability. Lip liners are hard wax pencils that give the lips definition and fullness and keep lipstick from bleeding around the mouth area. Lip sealers are clear coatings that go on over lipstick to keep the color in place longer. These can be either water-base or oil-base preparations

Makeup Remover

What goes on the face must eventually come off, especially during the evening cleansing process. Makeup remover is designed to remove makeup from the face and eye areas. Water-base cosmetics may be removed easily with a good facial cleanser designed for the skin type and water. Oil-base cosmetics, however, present a more difficult problem and require the use of specially formulated products for removal.

Like other skin care products, makeup removers are formulated for specific skin types. Lipid-base makeup removers contain oils and are recommended for use on dry skin to remove oil-base makeup. Detergent-base makeup removers contain detergents and water and are recommended for use on normal and oily skin to remove water-base makeup.

Sunscreens

Although not a type of makeup in the sense of the products mentioned above, sunscreens are a necessary part of any skin care program. Today, they are often included in cosmetics and skin treatment products. When cosmetics that do not contain sunscreens are applied, and the user is going to be exposed to sunlight, a sunscreen should be used after the moisturizer and before the foundation are applied. Sunscreens promote skin care and good health, and as such, they are included for discussion in this chapter.

THE SUN AND BLACK SKIN

The sun is a source of life for all organisms on this planet. Humans could not exist without it. In addition to providing energy, light and heat, the sun also serves as a source of vitamin D. However, the sun also presents dangers. It is a powerful source of ultraviolet (UV) radiation, which can damage the structure of the skin.

Although we cannot live without the sun, we must be ever aware of its inherent dangers!

The UV radiation from the sun is generated in three bands, measured in nanometers (nm), that is, millions of cycles per second. The first part of the UV energy spectrum is the UV-A band, which extends from 400 to 320 nm. This is the tanning region, where the melanocytes in the skin darken to help prevent damage. The second part of the spectrum is the UV-B band, which extends from 320 to 290 nm. This is the erythemal, or burning region, which causes sunburn. The third part is the UV-C band, which extends from 290 to 200 nm. This is the germicidal region, which is mostly absorbed by the ozone layer in the atmosphere. With the continued depletion of the ozone layer, however, these rays pose an increasing threat to life itself.

All three bands of UV radiation penetrate the skin and are potentially dangerous. Overexposure to UV radiation dries out the skin and destroys its elasticity, resulting in wrinkling and premature aging. Many of the harmful effects of the sun occur over a long period of time. Considerable evidence indicates that long-term exposure to the sun can lead to certain forms of skin cancer. It can be truly said that this is one area where the sins of youth reap their reward in later years.

However, even over the short term, overexposure to the sun is harmful. It causes the skin to burn, leading to redness, soreness, and discomfort. Severe sunburn can cause pain and nausea and, if not treated properly, can become infected. In view of the dangers of sun overexposure, the Environmental Protection Agency (EPA) and the National Weather Service

(NWS) have developed a UV exposure index as a measure of how quickly skin can be damaged by exposure to UV radiation given the atmospheric changes. This index is summarized in Table 6-1. The current index number is disseminated to local radio and television stations on a daily basis.

There is a popular misconception that black skin does not suffer from sunburn. This is not true! Although it is true that the increased melanin content of black skin provides some protection from UV radiation, the fact is that black skin is just as susceptible to sunburn as any other skin. Overexposure to the sun can cause burning, discomfort, premature aging, discoloration, and skin cancer in people with black skin.

Don't believe the misconception that black skin cannot be sunburned!

Sunscreens are just as important for the protection of black skin as they are for skin of any color. These products, although dispensed by over-the-counter sales, are classified as drugs by the Food and Drug Administration (FDA). As such, they are more tightly regulated than cosmetic products. Many different brands of sunscreens are available on the market. Each had to meet at least minimum FDA standards before being sold.

There are two types of sunscreen: physical agents and chemical agents. The physical agents, such as zinc oxide and titanium dioxide, are more properly called sun blocks because they reflect sunlight away from the body. These products tend to block both UV-A and UV-B radiation and, so, are more effective than chemical agent sunscreens, but on black skin, they tend to leave an ashy look to the skin. However, new formulations that prevent the ashiness are coming on the market. These products will allow more people with black skin to use sunscreens and sun blocks.

Chemical agents, such as para-aminobenzoic acid (PABA), however, work by absorbing the UV radiation. Most of these products absorb the more harmful UV-B rays while letting much of the UV-A radiation penetrate. As a result, the chemical agents tend to be less effective than the physical agents. In addition, many people develop allergic reactions to the sunscreen ingredients.

EPA/NWS Ultraviolet Index Ratings[*]

0 to 2   **Minimal UV**

Skin can be harmed with as little as 1 hour of unprotected exposure.

3 to 4   **Low UV**

Skin can be harmed with as little as 45 minutes of unprotected exposure.

5 to 6   **Moderate UV**

Skin can be harmed with as little as 30 minutes of unprotected exposure.

7 to 9   **High UV**

Skin can be harmed with as little as 15 minutes of unprotected exposure. EPA/NWS recommendations are to limit time in the sun at midday.

10+   **Very High UV**

Skin can be harmed with as little as 10 minutes of unprotected exposure. Maximum risk of burn and severe skin damage. EPA/NWS recommendations are to limit time in the sun from 10:30 AM to 3:30 PM.

[*] The UV index does not give specific corrections on time for black skin. Black skin has a certain level of protection because of the concentration and distribution of pigment cells. It is presumed that black skin can tolerate more sun for longer periods of time than white skin. Future studies will quantify this time differential.

Sunscreens, regardless of type, do not eliminate the danger of overexposure to the sun. They only extend the time a person may expose the skin to the sun before burning begins. As a measure of effectiveness, sunscreens are rated by their sun protection factor (SPF) numbers, which range from 2 to 50. So, for example, if a person whose unprotected skin would ordinarily burn after 10 minutes of exposure uses a sunscreen with an SPF of 15, he or she would be able to stay in the sun 15 times longer, or for 150 minutes, without burning.

The higher the SPF, the longer the exposure allowed and the more effective the sunscreen is. Most dermatologists agree that a sunscreen with an SPF of 15 provides the optimum protection. Products with an SPF rating of 2 to 4 give minimal protection from sunburn while allowing considerable tanning. Products with an SPF rating of 8 to 15 allow virtually no tanning but give considerably more protection from burning. Products with a higher SPF do not necessarily increase the protection greatly. For example, a product with an SPF of 2 blocks 50% of the UV radiation. A product with an SPF of 15 blocks 93% of the UV radiation. This is a considerable increase. But a product with an SPF of 34 blocks 97% of the UV radiation. As can be seen, the effectiveness of the sunscreen does not greatly increase above an SPF of 15. Products with an SPF higher than 15 also pose more of a potential risk for skin irritation or allergic reaction.

Be aware of the SPF number of sunscreens. Up to a point, the higher the SPF number the longer the exposure allowed and the more effective the sunscreen is.

Sunscreens are available as creams, lotions, and gels. Regardless of form, most sunscreens need to be reapplied at intervals, especially if they are worn while swimming. Gels are removed by perspiration more easily than other forms and may need to be reapplied more frequently. Gels, however, are preferred for people with oily or acne-prone skin. Regardless of form or brand, the manufacturer's directions for use should be followed. Use should be discontinued if an allergic reaction develops.

Chapter 7

Products for Black Skin Care

G*ood products are essential* to good skin care. Although skin care treatments can be given without the aid of machinery, they are virtually impossible to give without using some type of product formulated for some aspect of skin care.

For the most part, skin care products are not ethnic specific, that is, most products on the market can be used on black skin as well as white skin. However, some products have been specially formulated for use on black skin. These include products such as skin toners, which are used to lighten skin and even out coloration.

Many excellent skin care products are on the market, as well as many that are not so good. The esthetician or the consumer has to make intelligent choices from a sometimes dazzling array of materials and has to cut through the clutter and hype of advertising claims.

It is important to understand the products used in skin care. It is necessary to know what is in those products, why those things are there, and what effect they have. It is also necessary to know what products are available, and under what situations they are of most use. It is important to know enough about just about all of the various products on the market to be able to answer clients' questions. In today's marketplace, it is not enough to know how to do things. It is also necessary to know why those things are done.

REVIEW OF CHEMISTRY

All life on earth depends on chemistry. Without chemicals and chemical processes, there would be no existence at all. Chemistry can be loosely divided into two branches—inorganic and organic. *Organic chemistry* is concerned with compounds that contain carbon, the essential component for all living things. *Inorganic chemistry* is concerned with compounds that do not contain carbon, essentially all nonliving things. The boundaries are rather loose, though. Water (H_2O) is an inorganic compound as is air, which is a compound of oxygen, nitrogen, and small amounts of other gases. Gasoline, a hydrocarbon, is an organic compound, as is acetone. Hydrocarbons, that is, substances that contain carbon and hydrogen, are among the most important organic compounds. Skin care products fall into both categories. Some are organic compounds and some are inorganic compounds.

In addition, *biochemistry* is a subbranch of organic chemistry and deals with the chemical processes in living organisms. Amino acids, proteins, carbohydrates, and vitamins are examples of biochemicals.

Chemistry, regardless of branch, is the study of matter, the fundamental materials of the world, and its three states—solids, the ground we walk on; liquid, the water we drink; and gas, the air we breathe. Everything consists of one of these three forms of matter.

Matter consists of *elements*, which can exist singly or together in mixtures and compounds. There are 105 elements known although relatively few exist in great abundance. The human body, for example, consists primarily of three—carbon, oxygen, and hydrogen. There are other elements in the body, but they occur in small amounts. Table 7-1 lists the elements.

Mixtures consist of two or more elements intermingled physically but not chemically. Each element keeps its own characteristics. Take for example, salt and pepper. If they are mixed together, the result is a salt and pepper mixture that could be separated if someone wanted to get a pair of tweezers and a magnifying glass and take the time to do it. But the salt is still salt and the pepper is still pepper. *Compounds,* on the other hand, consist of two or more elements that combine chemically to form a different substance. The initial elements cannot be separated physically. Water is a good example. Water consists of two atoms of hydrogen (H) and one atom of oxygen (O)—two gases that combine to form the liquid compound, water (H_2O). The two elements have become something else. The hydrogen and the oxygen have both lost their original identities. Salt (NaCl) is a compound consisting of one atom of sodium (Na) and one atom of chlorine (Cl).

Elements differ from one another in their atomic structure. Each one consists of *atoms,* which are the smallest unit of the element that can combine with other elements. Atoms consist of subatomic particles—*protons* and *neutrons* in the core or nucleus of the atom, and *electrons* in orbit around the nucleus. The number of protons determines the characteristics of the element, thus its identity.

Molecules are combinations of atoms bound tightly together. The atoms can be alike or different. One molecule of oxygen, for example, consists of two atoms of oxygen. One molecule of water consists of one atom of oxygen and two atoms of hydrogen.

This information is fine in theory, but why is it important? It is important because it explains how and why the products used in skin care work. The esthetician as well as the consumer will work with solid, liquid, and gaseous products. Some of the products will be mixtures; some will be compounds. The size of the molecules of the product determines whether or not it will penetrate into the skin.

Matter—whether solid, liquid, or gas—comprises the fundamental materials of our world.

A basic understanding of chemistry is necessary to understand how cosmetic products work on the skin.

TABLE 7-1

Elements

Name	Symbol	Atomic Number	Atomic Weight	Name	Symbol	Atomic Number	Atomic Weight
Actinium*	Ac	89	227	Erbium	Er	68	167.3
Aluminum	Al	13	27	Europium	Eu	63	152
Americum*	Am	95	243	Fermium*	Fm	100	253
Antimony	Sb	51	121.8	Fluorine**	F	9	19
Argon	Ar	18	39.9	Francium*	Fr	87	223
Arsenic	As	33	74.9	Gadolinium	Gd	64	157.3
Astatine*	At	85	210	Gallium	Ga	31	69.7
Barium	Ba	56	137.3	Germanium	Ge	32	72.6
Berkelium*	Bk	97	247	Gold	Au	79	197
Beryllium	Be	4	9	Hafnium	Hf	72	178.5
Bismuth	Bi	83	209	Haxxxdum*	Ha	105	260
Boron	B	5	10.8	Helium	He	2	4
Bromine	Br	35	79.9	Holmium	Ho	67	165
Cadmium	Cd	48	112.4	Hydrogen	H	1	1
Calcium**	Ca	20	40.1	Indium	In	49	114.8
Californium*	Cf	98	249	Iodine**	I	53	126.9
Carbon	C	6	12	Iridium	Ir	77	192.2
Cerium	Ce	58	140.1	Iron**	Fe	26	55.9
Cesium	Cs	55	132.9	Krypton	Kr	36	83.8
Chlorine**	Cl	17	35.5	Lanthanum	La	57	138.9
Chromium**	Cr	24	52	Lawrencium*	Lw	103	257
Cobalt**	Co	27	58.9	Lead	Pb	82	207.2
Copper**	Cu	29	63.5	Lithium	Li	3	7
Curium*	Cm	96	247	Lutetium	Lu	71	175
Dysprosium	Dy	66	162.5	Magnesium**	Mg	12	24.3
Einsteinium*	Es	99	254	Manganese**	Mn	25	54.9

Name	Symbol	Atomic Number	Atomic Weight	Name	Symbol	Atomic Number	Atomic Weight
Mendelevium*	Md	101	256	Rutherfordium*	Rf	104	257
Mercury	Hg	80	200.6	Samarium	Sm	62	150.4
Molybdenum**	Mo	42	95.9	Scandium	Sc	21	45
Neodymium	Nd	60	144.2	Selenium**	Se	34	79
Neon	Ne	10	20.2	Silicon	Si	14	28.1
Neptunium*	Np	93	237	Silver	Ag	47	107.9
Nickel	Ni	28	58.7	Sodium**	Na	11	23
Niobium	Nb	41	92.9	Strontium*	Sr	38	87.6
Nitrogen	N	7	14	Sulfur**	S	16	32
Nobelium*	No	102	253	Tantalum	Ta	73	180.9
Osmium	Os	76	190.2	Technetium*	Tc	43	99
Oxygen	O	8	16	Tellurium	Te	52	127.6
Palladium	Pd	46	106.4	Terbium	Tb	65	158.9
Phosphorus**	P	15	31	Thallium	Tl	81	204.4
Platinum	Pt	78	195.1	Thorium	Th	90	232
Plutonium*	Pu	94	242	Thulium	Tm	69	168.9
Polonium*	Po	84	210	Tin	Sn	50	118.7
Potassium**	K	19	39.1	Titanium	Ti	22	47.9
Praseodymium	Pr	59	140.9	Tungsten	W	74	183.9
Promethium*	Pm	61	147	Uranium*	U	92	238
Protactinium*	Pa	91	231	Vanadium**	V	23	50.9
Radium*	Ra	88	226	Xenon	Xe	54	131.3
Radon*	Rn	86	222	Ytterbium	Yb	70	173
Rhenium	Re	75	186.2	Yttrium	Y	39	89
Rhodium	Rh	45	102.9	Zinc**	Zn	30	65.4
Rubidium	Rb	37	85.5	Zirconium	Zr	40	91.2
Ruthenium	Ru	44	101.1				

* Radioactive elements.
** Elements important to nutrition.

When different substances are mixed, a chemical reaction occurs. It is this reaction that creates the new substance, called the product. This product can be another chemical substance, or it can be energy in the form of heat, as in the digestion process, or electricity, as in a car battery. Estheticians are most concerned with oxidation-reduction reactions and neutralization reactions. Most biologic processes are examples of oxidation-reduction reactions. Neutralization reactions do just what they imply. They neutralize the actions of acids and bases.

Acids and *bases* are among the most important chemicals the esthetician works with. Many of the products used in skin care have either acidic or basic properties. Acids have a sour taste and turn litmus paper red. Bases, or alkalies, have a bitter taste and a slippery feel and turn litmus paper blue. Acids and bases can also be classified as either organic or inorganic. Hydrochloric acid (HCl), secreted by the stomach in the process of digestion, and sulfuric acid (H_2SO_4), found in car batteries, are inorganic acids. Phenol (HOC_6H_5), used in chemical skin peels, as well as the alpha-hydroxy acids, are organic acids. Caustic soda (NaOH) and ammonia (NH_3) are inorganic bases. Nicotine ($C_{10}H_{14}N_2$) is an organic base.

Although it is possible to tell whether a substance is acidic or alkaline with an indicator like litmus paper, that test does not tell how acidic or alkaline the substance is. The quantitative measure of acidity or alkalinity is pH. Simply speaking, pH is a logarithmic scale that measures the degree of acidity or alkalinity. The scale is measured from 0 to 14. From 0 to 7 is acidic; 7 is neutral; and from 7 to 14 is alkaline. But remember that this is a logarithmic scale, not linear, so 6 is 100% or twice as acid as 7; 5 is twice as acid as 6, and so on. The same ratio holds true in the other direction. Table 7-2 illustrates pH.

A few notable points here. Pure water is neutral. Normal skin has a pH of about 5.5. Extremely dry skin has a pH of about 3. Both are acidic. Extremely oily skin, on the other hand, has a pH of 9, meaning it is alkaline. This is a great concept. All that is necessary to determine the skin type of a client is to measure the pH. Unfortunately, it is not that simple. pH is hard to measure accurately without very expensive and highly technical

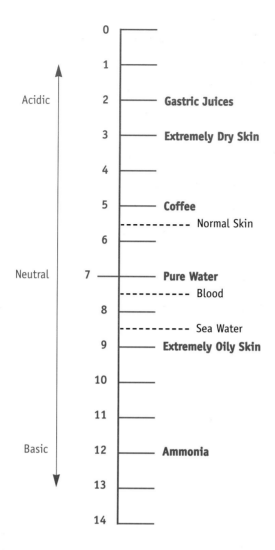

Table 7-2
pH chart

laboratory equipment. The concept is important nonetheless, because many of the products used rely on their acidity or alkalinity, measured by pH, to do their work.

Solutions are important, particularly liquid solutions. A *solution* is a homogeneous compound, that is, the molecules of the components are mingled uniformly. Although most of the solutions estheticians work with are liquid, a solution can also be a gas, as the air we breathe, or a solid, as in a metal alloy. Solutions consist of a *solute,* the substance being dissolved, and a *solvent,* the substance that dissolves the solute. Products use many different solvents, including alcohols, acids, and oils, but the most commonly used solvent in skin care products is water.

When it comes to solvents, attention centers on VOCs—volatile organic compounds from petroleum-based solvents, and their release into the atmosphere. They give the smell to products like nail polish removers. The Environmental Protection Agency (EPA) has virtually banned VOCs from the marketplace. Although their focus has been on industry, they may start monitoring businesses like beauty salons as well. Many manufacturers are looking at alternative solvents that will not release VOCs into the air.

> **It is probably only a matter of time until the EPA monitors the use of VOCs in businesses such as salons.**

When two liquids mix readily, they are said to be *miscible*. When they do not, they are said to be *immiscible*. Oils are not soluble in water; that is, oil and water do not mix. So when you have a product made with an oily component and a watery component, the manufacturer has to use a substance to keep the two phases from separating. That substance is called an *emulsifier*.

Remember the earlier discussion about the difference between compounds and mixtures. Solutions are compounds. In a liquid product when the molecules of the components do not intermingle but stay separate, the product is a heterogeneous mixture. When the particles are relatively large, the product is called a *suspension*. When they are relatively small, it is called a *colloid*. When a suspension or colloidal mixture sits on the shelf, the particles tend to settle to the bottom of the container. To overcome this, the manufacturer uses a dispersing agent to keep the particles in suspension and evenly distributed throughout the mixture.

Water is a marvelous substance. Only air is more important to human existence. A human can exist for weeks without food, but will die after being deprived of water for only a few days. Water is important to the body. It is important to the manufacture of most skin care products because it is the most commonly used solvent.

> **Water is vital to human existence!**

Water is not only a product component; it can be the product. When the esthetician uses the vaporizer, they are using the steam as a product.

When they rinse the cleanser from the client's face, they are using the water as a product.

Pure water, that is, water that contains nothing but the proper mix of hydrogen and oxygen, has a pH of 7 and is absolutely neutral. However, the only time water is pure is when it is distilled or deionized. Natural water, as it comes out of the ground, is never pure. It contains dissolved minerals. The content and quantity of these minerals depend on the area the water comes from. In addition, municipal water is treated and contains chemicals such as chlorine and fluorine. Sea water has more minerals yet and is discussed later.

Calcium and magnesium are the most commonly found minerals dissolved in water. When water contains these minerals, it is known as hard water. Hard water keeps suds from forming in soap, causes rings around bathtubs, and leaves mineral deposits around heating elements. This is the reason the manufacturer of the vaporizer recommends the use of distilled water to generate the steam.

Manufacturers usually use distilled or deionized water to make their products. The water in the salon should be checked for hardness. Hardness is measured in grains per gallon. If the water measures more than about 16 grains per gallon, the salon operator should seriously consider putting a water softener in the system. It will probably pay for itself in no time.

A water softener uses a deionization process that is more limited than the process used by manufacturers. In a water softener, the water passes over ion exchange beads that swap the metal mineral ions for sodium ions. The machines are regenerated with salt. At the same time, a filter should be installed to remove impurities such as iron, which is responsible for the red streaks sometimes found in laundry or in the toilet bowl.

PRODUCTS

The number of products available to the beauty industry is staggering. There are literally thousands of chemical products of various types, all competing for the buyer's attention.

Product choice starts with a close look at what is available. First, products can be grouped according to categories, that is, what they are used for—facial masks, toners, nail polish removers, permanent wave lotions, and so on. Within many product categories are subcategories, such as cleansers for oily skin, shampoos for dry hair, or those formulated to meet different ethnic needs.

The major factor in product proliferation is competition. With rare exception, every type of product is made by more than one manufacturer, with the result that there may be 30 different cleansers to choose from—or 86 different shampoos—or 27 different moisturizers. Many of these products will be virtually identical except for the name on the package and the claims made by the manufacturer. How does one decide which to use? Which to sell?

It's not easy! But there is a logical way to approach the problem and a few very simple rules to keep in mind. First, consider what the product does. Each product has a purpose—a reason for being. This is expressed in its category. So the first thing to decide is what does the user want the product to do? Next, what is its function? If the product does not accomplish something, it is useless. No matter how expensive it is. No matter how attractively it is packaged. No matter how much it has been promoted.

Understand the product's purpose and function before you use it.

Product Categories

Skin care products can be separated by category. These are the categories most likely to be used every day.

- Cleansers rid the skin of dirt and other impurities, such as dead cells, makeup, and excess sebum. An effective cleanser cleans both the surface of the skin and the pores. It cleans thoroughly, without drying the skin excessively or stripping it of its protective oils. It rinses off the skin easily.

- Toners, fresheners, and astringents complete the cleaning process by removing cleanser residue and helping restore the acid mantle. They also refresh the skin. Toners are used on dry skin and do not contain alcohol or other drying ingredients. Fresheners are used on normal skin. Astringents are designed for use on oily skin and generally contain alcohol to help dissolve excess oil.

- Moisturizers and night creams prevent moisture loss from the skin and keep it moist. They also help protect the skin from the environment. They soften the skin and slow the effects of aging by keeping the skin moist. Moisturizers are designed primarily for daytime use. They deposit a thin film of water, oil, and emollient on the surface of the skin but do not penetrate the skin. The barrier formed by the moisturizer film holds the moisture in the skin.

- Night creams are similar to moisturizers. They also help retard moisture loss but also contain ingredients that help repair skin damage. These products, meant to be used at night while the body is resting, do penetrate to a limited degree. Their ingredients help restore cellular function and soothe and nourish the skin. Moisturizers can be covered with makeup, but night creams should be left uncovered.

- Eye and throat creams are products designed to provide nutrients and lubrication to those areas around the eyes and on the neck that have little natural oil of their own. These products are most useful with dry, aging skin.

- Masks are among the most useful of skin care products. There are many different types of masks, each formulated for a specific purpose. Tightening masks help tighten and tone sagging skin, drawing masks absorb excess oils, and moisturizing masks add moisture to the skin. Depending on its formulation, a mask can soothe the skin, oxygenate it and improve circulation, nourish, help clear blemishes, or reduce fine lines and wrinkles for a short period of time. Masks can be either hard or soft.

- Scrubs and peels are exfoliant products that basically work like supercleansers to remove dead skin cells and remove impurities from the pores while stimulating and improving the circulation of the skin. Scrubs contain small granules of mild abrasives that remove dirt and dead cells when they are rubbed off the skin. They leave the skin clean and glowing.

- Peels contain enzymes that digest the dead skin cells. They do not have an abrasive action. These enzymatic peels work on the surface of the skin and are safe to use. Chemical peels, however, remove layers of living skin and may be used only by dermatologists or other physicians.

- Treatment products fall into a broad category that covers all those products that help normalize the skin function and help heal skin problems. *Note:* the term is "help heal and normalize." Estheticians do not cure skin conditions. Estheticians are not physicians. There is no faster way for an esthetician to get into deep trouble than by offering cures for anything.

Remember: Estheticians do not *cure* conditions. Estheticians are not physicians!

- Special purpose products cover a wide range of products designed to accomplish specific tasks. These can include such items as oil absorbers, which are made to absorb excess oil from the skin. They can include skin toners, which are designed to lighten the skin and even out skin coloration. If someone has uncovered a need for a product that performs a specific task, it is almost a sure thing that some company has developed a product to meet that need.

The same story applies for hair and nail care products—shampoos, conditioners, permanent wave lotions, colorants, nail polish removers, nail polishes, and on and on. No matter what services are offered, a complete category of products will help provide that service.

Product States

Next, consider the product state. What form does the product take? This is important because it affects how the product is used. Products are available in a number of different forms—liquids, creams, lotions, gels, solids, aerosols, and so on. Liquids flow freely and are pourable. They tend to be clear. Creams tend to be thicker and are usually emulsified and are generally opaque. Creams are usually spreadable. A pourable cream is a lotion, which is not as thick. Gels are thick and sticky, with a jelly-like consistency. They are not usually emulsified and can be clear or transparent. Solids can be loose and free-flowing, like powder, or they can be bound particles, as in sticks. They can vary in texture and in consistency. Some solid products are used in that form. Others are mixed with water or other liquid for use, as, for example, a wheat germ mask, which comes as dry particles of wheat germ that are mixed with warm water to make a spreadable paste. Other solids are heated to change them into a liquid form for use, like a paraffin mask, where the solid paraffin wax has to be heated to about 134°, where it will flow onto the skin, before it can be used. As it cools down on the client's skin, it becomes a solid again. Aerosols let the user apply the product as a mist or a foam. In a mist, the product is broken into tiny droplets and dispersed by a propellant. In a foam, the product mixes with the propellant to form a fluffy, light, aerated mass.

You cannot consider the product contents or function without also considering how it is packaged. In many cases, the chemicals in the product will determine its form and its packaging. No matter what form the product takes, it has to be packaged in some way. The packaging is an important part of the product. It lets the product be stored. It protects the product. It identifies the product. And it allows access to the product. Especially for retail sales, it makes the product attractive.

Like the products themselves, the packaging can take a number of forms—bottles, jars, cans, boxes, tubes, ampules, and so on. Bottles are used for pourable liquids and lotions. Jars and cans are for creams and loose solids. Boxes hold bound solids and tubes contain pastes and gels.

Ampules are small hermetically sealed glass tubes that contain a concentrated active ingredient.

Regardless of type, the package performs a number of functions. It has to keep the product clean and sanitary, so it must be relatively impervious to the outside. In the case of just about all but bound particle solids, the package should not let in air, moisture, or contaminants, nor should it let the product leak out. If the product is sensitive to light, the package should be opaque or transparent dark brown or green. The package should be reclosable. With ampules, for example, once one is opened, the entire contents must be used.

The package should allow ready access to the contents, that is, it should make the product easy to use. If the user cannot get the product out of the container in the amount needed when needed, the package is not functional.

The key product questions still remain, however. What is in the product? What ingredients does it contain? And even more importantly, what do these ingredients do? What do they accomplish?

PRODUCT INGREDIENTS

All products consist of one or more ingredients. Hopefully, the manufacturer has chosen those ingredients to formulate the best possible product. Regardless of how many ingredients may be in a product, each should contribute something to its functioning. All ingredients should be compatible, that is, they have to work together and not fight each other. They also should be mixed correctly.

Ingredients can be divided into two main groups—active ingredients and formulation aids. Active ingredients are substances that actually do the work the product is supposed to do—the cleansing, the toning, the normalization, and so on. Formulation aids are substances that help the active ingredients do their work and provide important characteristics to the product.

Active Ingredients. Active ingredients are the substances that do the actual work. In terms of composition, they may be natural, that is, derive from animal, vegetable, or mineral components, or they may be synthetic, that is, manufactured. Regardless of their composition, they are all chemical. In terms of quantity, they may or may not be the major ingredients in the product. In fact, they will rarely be the major ingredients in the product. With few exceptions, there will be more formulation aids in a product than active ingredients.

Active ingredients in products may be natural or synthetic. They are all, however, chemical and are the substances that do the actual work of the product.

- Cleansing agents, for example, soaps, detergents, skin cleansers, shampoos, do the actual work of cleaning the skin or hair by softening dirt and loosening its hold on the skin or hair so it can be rinsed away. Cleansers include sodium laureth sulfate and lauroamphocarboxyglycinate.

- Emollients soften and soothe by lubricating the skin. They also help hydrate the skin. There are a great many emollients. Some of the more popular include aloe vera, a botanical agent; lanolin, an animal agent; and cetyl acetate and myristal myristate, synthetic agents.

- Exfoliants can be considered supercleansers. They soften and remove (or aid in the removal of) dead skin cells from the surface of the skin. The AHAs, alpha-hydroxy acids, are currently widely used.

- Healing agents promote healing or soothing of the skin, provide antiseptic properties, and reduce or help prevent inflammation. Commonly used healing agents include herbs such as aloe, chamomile, and yarrow; vitamins such as biotin and retinol; minerals such as zinc oxide; and synthetic materials such as urea.

- Moisturizing agents help the skin absorb and retain moisture. Aloe and safflower oil are examples.

• Protectants do just what the name implies. They protect the skin from harm. Sunscreens are an example.

Formulation Aids. When it comes to formulation aids, the list is even longer and more varied. In almost any given product, there will be more formulation aids than active ingredients. They are just as important as the active ingredients. Without these substances, the product would lack many of the properties that make it work and, sometimes more importantly, make it easy to use or make it marketable.

Most products contain more formulation aids than active ingredients.

• Antioxidants prevent spoilage caused by exposure to oxygen. Commonly used antioxidants include tocopherol (vitamin E) and benzoic acid. Some formulation aids can also function as active ingredients. Antioxidants, for example, can scavenge free radicals from the skin, and thus, act as protectants or healing agents.

• Binders hold the ingredients together and increase the consistency of the formulation. Sorbitol and glycerin are often used for this purpose.

• Buffers control the level of acidity or alkalinity during formulation by preventing wide swings in pH. Commonly used buffers include citric acid and calcium carbonate.

• Clarifiers remove unwanted materials to make them clear. Citric acid and tannin are commonly used.

• Colorants give the product its characteristic color. A wide variety of vegetable, animal, or mineral dyes or pigments are used. These may be used without specific government approval. Coal tar derivative dyes, however, must undergo a certification process before they can be used in skin and beauty care products. Certified colorants are listed as FD&C (food, drug and cosmetic) colors, which can be used in foods as well as in drugs and cosmetics; D&C colors, which cannot be used in food, but can be used in drugs or cosmetics; or ext. D&C colors, which may be used only for external use in drugs and cosmetics.

- Defoaming agents keep the ingredients from foaming during formulation. Simethicone is one of the most widely used defoamers. This chemical is the main active ingredient in many over-the-counter remedies for excess gas.

- Deodorizers eliminate unpleasant or unwanted smells. Chlorophyll and urea are often used for this purpose.

- Emulsifiers let oil and water be mixed together to form an emulsion. Commonly used emulsifiers include glyceryl stearate, polysorbate 80, and triethanolamine (TEA).

- Extenders increase the volume of the product and dilute the product. Water and petrolatum are two examples.

- Fixatives retard the vaporization of the components of fragrances, making the desired odors last longer. Musk and civet are commonly used as fixatives.

- Foaming agents are added to products, usually cleansers and shampoos, to make them foam during use. Dodecylbenzene sulfonic acid is one example.

- Fragrances give the product its characteristic odor. A wide variety of natural and synthetic fragrances are used. They operate on three levels. The first impression, or top-note, of the fragrance is the most volatile and vaporizes first. The major characteristics of the fragrance are in the second level, or body-note, which vaporizes more slowly. The third level, or bottom-note, is what is left after the volatile components of the fragrance have vaporized. Fragrances are made up of complex blends of ingredients and are normally regarded as proprietary, that is, trade secrets, of manufacturers. They are the only ingredients in a product that do not have to be listed on the label.

- Humectants retard moisture loss in the product while it is in the container and also help trap moisture on the skin. Glycerin, sorbitol, and propylene glycol are widely used.

- Lubricants provide a coating on the skin to reduce friction and wear. Mineral oil, cocoa butter, and isopropyl myristate are common lubricants.

- Opacifiers make the product milky, so that light is not transmitted through it. Cetyl alcohol and stearyl alcohol are often used for this purpose.

- Preservatives kill harmful bacteria, fungi, and yeasts, increasing the shelf life of the product and keeping it safe to use. Isothiazolone, methyl paraben, and imidazolindyl urea are among the preservatives in the formulators' arsenal.

- Sequestering agents retard changes in the appearance of the product, especially in color or texture. Although they are a type of preservative, they work by chemical action as opposed to attacking microorganisms. Tetrasodium pyrophosphate (TSPP) and ethylenediamine tetraacetic acid (EDTA) are common sequestering agents.

- Solvents dissolve or disperse the other ingredients in a product. Water is the most common solvent. Alcohol, acetone, and methyl ethyl ketone are also used.

- Stabilizers maintain the equilibrium of the product and keep its characteristics from changing. Among the many stabilizers used in skin care products are borax, polysorbate 80, and cetyl alcohol.

- Surfactants reduce the surface tension of the product and allow the product to spread and penetrate more easily. They are also called wetting agents. Sodium laureth sulfate and dioctyl succinate are two of the most commonly used surfactants.

- Texturizers enhance the texture of products, that is, they make the products smoother. Calcium chloride and biotin are commonly used.

- Thickeners give body to the product. Among the commonly used thickeners are bentonite, carbomer 934, stearic acid, and cellulose gum.

- Vehicles are carriers for the other ingredients and in most cases, account for the largest portion of the product. Water is the most commonly used vehicle, although alcohol or other solvents are also used.

Product Labeling

By law, all cosmetic products must list all ingredients on the label, except for specific fragrances. Ingredients are listed in descending order according to the amount of the ingredient contained in the product. Actual amounts do not have to be listed.

Labels are important. In many ways, they are the primary source of information about a product and what goes into it. So it is important to know how to read product labels. For example, here is a list of ingredients on the Dr. Thrower Dry Skin Cleanser. According to the label, the cleanser contains: water, isopropyl palmitate, glycerin, stearic acid, TEA, cetyl alcohol, sodium lauryl sulfate, EDTA, methylparaben, propylparaben, diazolidinyl urea, carbomer, sodium benzoate, and fragrance.

Estheticians and consumers must know how to read product labels.

- Water, the ingredient present in the greatest quantity, is the vehicle. It carries the rest of the ingredients, dispersing them evenly throughout the product.

- Isopropyl palmitate is an emollient and moisturizer to soothe and soften the skin. It is derived from coconut or palm oil.

- Glycerin is a humectant that helps the skin retain water. It also helps the cleanser spread evenly.

- Stearic acid is an emulsifier and thickening agent. It is one of the main ingredients in soap.

- TEA (triethanolamine) is also an emulsifier. It helps adjust the pH of the cleanser.

- Cetyl alcohol acts as both an active ingredient and a formulation aid. As an active ingredient, it is an emollient that helps soothe and smooth the skin. As a formulation aid it is an emulsifier and a thickener.

- Sodium lauryl sulfate is the primary cleansing agent in the cleanser. It is a foaming agent and a dispersant and also acts as a surfactant.

- EDTA (ethylendiamine tetraacetic acid), methylparaben, propylparaben, diazolidinyl urea, and sodium benzoate are preservatives. Diazolidinyl urea is also a deodorizer and antiseptic.

- Carbomer is a cross-linking agent that stabilizes the emulsion and helps keep the particles in suspension.

- Fragrance gives the product a pleasant aroma.

Product Modes of Action

It is also necessary to understand the modes of action of the various products used. Products, and their ingredients, work in three ways—chemically, mechanically, and psychologically. All three modes are equally important to a product's effectiveness.

Products work chemically as they undergo chemical reactions with and within the body, as when a healing agent reacts with an inflammation to reduce the pain and soothe the skin or when a cleanser reacts with dirt and sebum to loosen their hold on the skin.

Products work mechanically as they coat the skin to trap moisture or develop heat from friction as they are rubbed onto the skin.

Products react psychologically as they make the client feel better and provide a sense of well-being. The products are comfortable and soothing. The psychological effects of the products used or the services provided should not be underestimated. After all, that is what a successful salon is really selling.

The psychological reaction to a product is equally as important as the chemical and mechanical reaction in a client.

Characteristics of a Good Product

What makes a product good? A good product has seven major attributes:

1. Effectiveness—it actually works and does what it is supposed to do.

2. Reliability—it works the same way every time; it can be counted on to do its job.

3. Ease of Use—it is easy to store, easy to apply, and easy to remove. It has clear, concise directions for best use. In short, it does not require more work than is necessary.

4. Cost effectiveness—it is affordable to use it in the salon. It has a long enough shelf life so it can be purchased in reasonable quantity and stored without spoilage. It gives excellent value for the money spent.

5. Safety—it will not harm clients or staff, as long as it is used properly and directions for use are followed.

6. Pleasant—it smells good, it looks good, and is enjoyable to use.

7. Salability—the operator can make a profit on the product.

THE FDA AND THE FTC

It is also important to understand the role of the Food and Drug Administration (FDA) and Federal Trade Commision (FTC). They are two federal agencies that greatly affect the beauty business. The FDA is responsible for monitoring the safety and effectiveness of cosmetics, food, and drugs and seeing that these products meet the standards of the Food, Drug and Cosmetic Act. It tests and approves products and has the authority to remove products from the marketplace. The agency can also challenge claims made by manufacturers about the products and can demand substantiation of those claims. It is also responsible for monitoring the truth and accuracy of claims made on packaging and on labels.

In the "alphabet soup" of governmental agencies, estheticians must understand the roles of the FDA and FTC.

The FTC enforces laws that prevent unfair competitive practices in business. It is also responsible for stopping the manufacture and sale of counterfeit products, which is a big problem in the beauty industry. Although the FTC does not get involved in products otherwise, it can demand substantiation for claims made in advertising.

One area the FDA gets involved with is defining the difference between a cosmetic and a drug. What is the difference? This is an important consideration for estheticians and consumers. Cosmetologists can use cosmetics on clients. They cannot use drugs. Drugs are the jealously and zealously guarded tools of the medical community.

In the most simple terms, *cosmetics* are products that remain on the surface of the skin or at most, penetrate only into the epidermal layer of the skin. *Pharmaceuticals* (drugs) penetrate into and beyond the dermal layer of the skin and are absorbed into the bloodstream. Cosmetics beautify. Drugs cure. Cosmetics do not significantly or permanently alter the skin's structure or function, or affect any body function beyond the skin. Drugs do significantly and permanently affect body functions.

All cosmetics are used topically, that is, they are applied to the surface of the skin. Drugs are used topically and are ingested, that is, they may be taken internally. But a cosmetic can contain ingredients that are classed as cosmetic when used in a beauty aid but classed as a drug when taken internally. Take, for example, salicylic acid, an ingredient in some skin cleansers. As the major ingredient of aspirin, taken internally, it cures a headache.

The key to the difference is skin penetration. Do cosmetic products actually penetrate into the skin? The answer is a qualified yes. While the skin is a relatively impermeable barrier, if the molecular structure of the product is small enough, it will penetrate the skin, at least into the epidermal layer. If the molecules are too large, the product will not penetrate. But a skin care product doesn't have to penetrate the skin to be effective. Most products are designed to work on the skin's surface and they do the job admirably.

The line between cosmetics and drugs has become thinner and thinner as new advances in technology have been made. It is important not to cross that line. Many cosmetic manufacturers are carefully walking that line now. In fact, many of the claims they make for their cosmetic products—if they were true—would have the FDA classify them as drugs.

The key to the difference between a drug and a cosmetic is skin penetration. In general, cosmetics remain on the surface of the skin or penetrate only into the epidermal layer. Drugs penetrate into the skin and are absorbed into the bloodstream.

PRODUCT CLAIMS—MYTHS AND MISCONCEPTIONS

It is vital to look at product claims carefully. Keep in mind that most manufacturers are ethical in their business dealings and genuinely try to make truthful claims about the products. In most cases, they actually believe the claims they make because they can show scientific proof that the claims are true. But they are driven by a need to generate a profit on the products and are pushed by competitive pressures to exploit fads in the cosmetics business and to show their products are better than the competition's.

The reader should keep an open mind and give the manufacturers the benefit of the doubt as to their integrity, but should take what they say with a grain of salt until the truth of the claims can be verified. Intelligent users should also know that miracles do not come in bottles or jars. There is an old adage that holds just as true with products. "If it sounds too good to be true, it isn't true."

What are some of the current fads in the beauty industry that are fueling product proliferation and claims for those products? And are those claims true or false? Or just misleading?

"Our products are all natural and chemical free." First, there's no such thing as a chemical-free product. Remember what was said before. Everything is chemical, whether it is natural or not. All matter is composed of chemicals. As to the all-natural claim—just because something contains herbs does not make it automatically natural. Read the label. Are there preservatives in it? Is the herbal content from herbal extracts? What about the other ingredients?

Even if something were to be all natural, that is no guarantee of quality or effectiveness. Some of the most virulent poisons are all natural. Poison ivy, for example, is all natural.

"Our product is not tested on animals." This claim is probably true, but just what does it mean. All the manufacturer is saying is that the finished product was not tested on animals. However, many of the ingredients in the product have been tested on animals. If they were not, the FDA would not allow their use. Some ingredients fall into an FDA classification GRAS, or generally recognized as safe. Others, however, have to undergo rigorous testing before the FDA will let them be used. Up to now, at least, the FDA will recognize as valid only tests conducted on animals. So, is the manufacturer's claim true? Yes. Is it meaningful? Probably not.

"Our product is hypoallergenic." All this means is that the product does not contain a fragrance. Countless tests and studies have shown that the major cause of allergic reactions in cosmetic products result from the fragrances they contain. Removing the fragrance lessens the likelihood of allergic reactions and the manufacturer can call the product "hypoallergenic." It does not mean that the client cannot have an allergic reaction to the product. If the client is allergic to anything in the product, they will have an aller-

Hypoallergenic does not necessarily mean your client will not have an allergic reaction to some ingredient in the product. Hypoallergenic only means the product has no fragrance.

gic reaction. This is the reason patch tests should be conducted, even with hypoallergenic products.

"Our products fight aging." The single greatest cause of premature skin aging, which is what is most often seen, is overexposure to UV radiation, whether from the sun or from a tanning booth. If the skin is shielded from the radiation, aging will be retarded. If a manufacturer puts a sunscreen in the product, the FDA allows the claim that the product is anti-aging. As a result, it is getting harder and harder to find cosmetic products without a sunscreen in them, even when the only reason for that ingredient is to support the claim of anti-aging. After all, why is it necessary to put a sunscreen in a night cream?

"Our products are alcohol free." When most people think of alcohol, they think of rubbing alcohol or liquor. But alcohol takes many forms. Cetyl alcohol, for example, is a waxy solid that has none of the characteristics of its more widely known cousins. Unfortunately, alcohol is currently out of fashion in cosmetics, with the result that many manufacturers are touting alcohol-free products, even when no alcohol would have been used in the product in the first place. Keep in mind, though, that alcohols and their derivatives are important in cosmetic manufacture. Aldehydes, ketones, organic acids, and esters are all made from alcohol. So a product may be alcohol free, but ingredients may have come from alcohol.

"Our products are preservative free." They better not be! Not if the user expects to use them safely or keep them stored for any length of time. Preservatives are essential for just about any type of product in use. They are what keep funny looking little things from growing in the bottle while it sits on the shelf. The only ways a manufacturer can keep from adding preservatives to products are to either keep them in refrigerated storage, keep them in sterile containers such as ampules, or to use ingredients that have built-in antiseptic properties. Another note, the more natural a product is, the more susceptible it is to microbial contamination, and the more it needs a preservative.

"Our products get rid of unsightly wrinkles." This is not totally true. No cosmetic product can permanently erase wrinkles. The best they can do is to make wrinkles less evident or to hide them temporarily.

"Our product contains alpha-hydroxy acids." The alpha-hydroxy acids, AHAs, are the current industry darlings. Virtually every manufacturer has jumped on this bandwagon. The term alpha-hydroxy acid covers a variety of organic acids derived from fruit and other sugars. The most commonly used AHAs are glycolic acid from sugar cane, lactic acid from milk, and citric acid from citrus fruits. Others include malic acid from apples and tartaric acid from wine. They represent a class of chemicals that seem to have outstanding emollient and soothing effects on the skin and are excellent exfoliants. Like any product, though, they need to be used properly and carefully. They are acids, and like any acid, can burn the skin if not used correctly.

The AHAs do a great job, but for best results they have to be used in fairly high concentration, which limits their use by anyone other than physicians. In cosmetic preparations, the concentration is limited by law. As a result, the effectiveness of these products is limited, although they are valuable tools in the hands of a competent esthetician. The problem is that they are so popular right now that manufacturers are making products containing AHAs, even in products such as cleansers, which are rinsed off the skin before the AHA has much chance to do any good at all. Here's an example of a potentially good product being overcome by too much hype.

Chapter 8

Herbs, Essential Oils, and Sea Products

H*erbs, essential oils, and sea water* and products from the sea are widely used ingredients in skin care products. A wide variety of these ingredients are available to the skin care product manufacturer. Each of these ingredients has specific uses. As a result, it is necessary to have a basic understanding of the principles involved in these products because of their impact on the care of the skin.

HERBS

The use of herbs (i.e., plant materials) has its roots in antiquity. Every culture, even the most primitive, has a history of herbal medicine. Today, herbs are widely used throughout the world. Whether used as spices, cosmetics, or medicine, herbs play an important part in everyday life. Although the medical use of herbs has declined in our modern technological societies in favor of allopathic medicine, which relies on synthetic drugs, herbs remain valuable homeopathic remedies.

Hundreds of different herbs are used both singly and in combinations. Collectively, these herbs have a variety of properties. They soothe or stimulate, moisten or dry, tighten or ease. They heal, alleviate pain, dispel gas, cleanse, and purify the blood. They arouse or diminish sexual desire. They are antiseptic, antibiotic, and disinfectant. They increase perspiration or decrease it. The list could go on and on.

As medicines, herbs detoxify, normalize, or build. Detoxifying herbs eliminate poisons from the body and help purify it. Normalizing herbs help correct imbalances in bodily functions that result in illness; thus, they let the body heal itself as opposed to synthetic drugs, which alleviate symptoms but may not eliminate the underlying cause of the illness. The building herbs strengthen the various organs of the body to help prevent further illnesses.

As homeopathic remedies, herbs work slowly. Allopathic remedies, that is, synthetic drugs, work quickly. As an analogy, consider an illness as a mountain. There are two ways to level a mountain. It can be eroded by the action of rain and the elements slowly but gently, with no traces left or it can be blasted apart with dynamite, quickly but roughly, with rubble strewn about. Although they work slowly, herbs are thorough yet gentle and, for the most part, have few undesirable side effects. Synthetic drugs, on the other hand, work rapidly, but are rougher on the body's systems and can have a number of undesirable side effects.

Retinol A, for example, a widely used drug for treating acne, controls blemishes rapidly and effectively but has potentially harmful side effects, such as headache, nausea, and possible destruction of sebaceous glands. By careful use of skin care products that contain a variety of herbs, it is possible to control acne effectively, albeit more slowly, without side effects to the client. The drug treats the symptom of acne, the excess sebum. The herbs treat the underlying causes of acne and bring the body functions into balance so the reasons for the excess sebum are eliminated.

Admittedly, this example is overly simplified. It is important to remember that allopathic remedies are valuable and should be used when warranted. Always follow the advice of a physician.

Herbs are available from many sources. They may be picked in the wild, but this requires considerable time and expertise. Similarly, they may be grown in home gardens. This also requires time. For the esthetician, the more practical sources are the herb specialty stores and some manufacturers of skin care products.

Herbs are most effective when they are used fresh. The fresh plant consists of the root, stem, leaf, and in the case of the flowering plants, flower and fruit, and in the case of woody plants, bark. For a given herb, one or more parts of the plant may contain the active, or medicinal, ingredient. Fresh herbs must be used soon after they are picked because their effectiveness diminishes rapidly. For this reason, fresh herbs are harder to use.

To maintain long-term stability, herbs are often dried, then ground into powders for use. Although they lose some activity when dried, they remain efficacious for longer periods. They should be stored in dark, air-tight containers to prevent moisture absorption that could cause them to spoil.

> Although herbs are most effective when fresh, this is not always practical. Thus, herbs are often dried and ground into powders, allowing them to remain efficacious for longer periods.

Herbs may be prepared in a number of ways: as infusions, decoctions, poultices, fomentations, tinctures or ointments.

- An *infusion* is made by steeping the herb in boiling water, just as in making tea. (Herb teas are infusions.) The process of steeping extracts the vitamins and volatile ingredients from the plant. The liquid is then strained and can be taken internally or used externally.

- A *decoction* is similar to an infusion, except the herb is boiled in the water instead of being steeped. This process extracts the mineral salts and bitter principles from the plant. The liquid must be strained before using.

- A *poultice* is made by bruising or crushing the herb and mixing the pulpy mass with a hot liquid or gummy substance to make a paste. The paste can be applied directly to the skin or wrapped in a hot, moist towel and wrapped around the body part to be treated.

- A *fomentation* is made by soaking a towel in a hot infusion or decoction and applying it to the body part to be treated. Fomentations are less effective than poultices because the application of the active ingredient is less direct.

- A *tincture* is made by soaking the herb in alcohol. The alcohol extracts the active ingredient from the plant. Tinctures keep for long periods of time. Tinctures meant for internal use must be made with grain alcohol. Those meant for external use only may be made with other alcohols.

- An *ointment* is made by mixing the herb with a hot fat or petroleum jelly to make a thick cream or salve. The salve is spread on the area of the body to be treated. Ointments are for external use only.

Although herbs may be used both internally and externally, skin care is concerned only with the external applications.

Hundreds of herbs have application in skin care. It is beyond the scope of this chapter to cover any but the most commonly used plants. Different herbs have different properties and affect the skin in different ways. Some are astringent, some cleansing, some purifying, some healing. Some herbs tighten skin; others ease tightness; some stimulate; others soothe. Table 8-1 lists a number of commonly used herbs.

Many herbs perform more than one function. Also, many herbs work in synergy. Combining herbs produces effects far in excess of the effect of each herb individually. The sum of the herbal effectiveness is greater than the total of the parts.

Hundreds of herbs are available for use either alone or in combination to treat the skin.

Because of their effectiveness, a number of herbs are used in commercial skin care preparations. Among the most commonly used herbs are:

Acacia, also known as gum arabic, is a small tree common to tropical Africa. The useful part of the plant is the gum that exudes from the stem. Acacia soothes and softens skin. As a gum, it often serves as a binder for other ingredients in skin care preparations.

Almond is a tree grown in many parts of the world. The kernels of the nut are the most useful part of the plant. Almonds are emollients that help smooth rough skin while moisturizing. Ground almond meal makes a good cleansing scrub.

Aloe vera is a spiny, cactus-like plant native to east and south Africa, although it is cultivated in other tropical areas. The leaves, from which the gel is extracted, are used. Aloe is healing and soothing. It helps reduce inflammation. It moisturizes the skin and helps slow the outward appearance of aging. This herb has become one of the most popular herbs used in skin care.

Arnica is a perennial plant found in the northern latitudes. The flowers and roots are the useful parts of the plant. Arnica helps skin function normally by stimulating circulation and helping remove waste materials. It is an astringent and aids in the healing process.

Balm, also known as balm mint, is a perennial plant found in the Mediterranean and Near East countries as well as in the United States. The leaves are the most important part, although most of the plant may be used as well. A member of the mint family, balm is, at the same time, both soothing and stimulating to the skin.

Birch, also called white birch, is a tree common to the northern United States and Canada. The bark is the most important part, although the young leaves may also be useful. The herb is soothing and healing and is an astringent. The active ingredient in birch bark is salicylic acid, the major component of aspirin.

Chamomile is a perennial plant found throughout Europe. The flowers are the important part of the plant. Chamomile softens and heals the skin and is an astringent. The active ingredient in chamomile is azulene, an anti-irritant and anti-inflammatory agent.

TABLE 8-1

Commonly Used Herbs

Herb	Properties	Remarks
Acacia (gum arabic)	astringent, healing	tightening, stimulating, nourishing
Almond	cleansing, moisturizing	good antiwrinkle agent, blackhead remover
Aloe	healing, soothing, moisturizing, softening	good for all types of skin, especially dry skin
Arnica	astringent, healing	good for circulation
Balm mint	soothing, stimulating	
Birch	astringent, healing	good on damaged and blemished skin
Chamomile	astringent, soothing, cleansing, anti-inflammatory	good for blackhead removal, good antiwrinkle agent
Coltsfoot	healing, soothing	good on couperose skin
Comfrey	healing, softening cell regenerator	good for blackhead removal and damaged skin
Cucumber	astringent, drying, tightening	good for oily skin
Echinacea	astringent, healing	
Elder	Healing, astringent, tightening	good for oily skin
Grape	Soothing, healing	good for dry skin

continued

Herb	Properties	Remarks
Horsetail	astringent, tightening, drying, stimulating	good for oily skin
Houseleek	healing, nourishing	good for blackhead removal and on blemished skin
Lady's mantle	astringent, drying, healing, cleansing, anti-inflammatory	good for oily skin, good antiwrinkle agent
Lemon	astringent, drying, healing, soothing	good for oily skin and blackhead removal
Marigold	healing, moisturizing, softening, soothing	good for circulation, good antiwrinkle agent, good for couperose skin
Marshmallow	healing, soothing, softening	good on damaged skin
Rosemary	astringent, cleansing, stimulating, antiseptic	good for circulation
Sage	astringent, healing, tightening, soothing	good for oily skin
St. John's wort	astringent, healing, antiseptic	
Witch hazel	astringent, drying, antiseptic	
Wild Oregon grape	purifying, healing	good for blemished skin
Yarrow	astringent, drying, stimulating	good for oily skin and blackhead removal

Coltsfoot is a perennial plant found in wet areas in the United States and Europe. The leaves and the flowers are the important parts. Coltsfoot soothes and heals the skin. It acts on the capillaries near the surface of the skin, making it good for use on couperose skin.

Comfrey is a perennial plant common to the United States and Europe. The roots are the most important part of the plant. Comfrey softens the skin and helps heal wounds and bruises. It also helps stimulate tissue growth. The active ingredient of comfrey is allantoin.

Cucumber, the fruit of the common garden plant, is an important plant for skin care. Cucumber juice is an astringent that softens, moisturizes, and nourishes the skin.

Echinacea, a midwestern perennial plant, has antiseptic properties and is useful as a blood purifier. Like all herbs that purify the blood, echinacea can be effective for use on skin conditions such as eczema and acne. The root is the part of the plant used.

Elder, a shrub native to many parts of the world in a variety of forms, has healing properties. An astringent, it stimulates circulation and tightens skin. Roots, leaves, and flowers all contribute to skin care.

Horsetail is an annual plant native to North and South America. The leaves have astringent properties. Horsetail is stimulating and drying and helps tighten the skin. It helps promote elasticity and rejuvenates the skin.

Houseleek, a perennial European plant, is astringent and cooling. Juice from the leaves is healing and soothing for a number of skin conditions.

Lady's mantle, a perennial plant found in damp areas in North America and Europe, is healing and anti-inflammatory. It is an astringent and natural cleanser. The entire plant can be used.

Lemon, the citrus fruit common to Florida and California, is an effective astringent and cleanser for the skin. It has healing and drying properties and helps hydrate surface cells. Pure lemon juice may be too acidic for direct application to the skin and should be diluted with water.

Marigold, also known as calendula, is an annual garden plant. The leaves and flowers have antiseptic and healing properties and help soften skin. Marigold helps detoxify and nourish skin cells.

Marshmallow is a plant found in waste areas in Europe and North America. It is a lubricant and softener for the skin and has healing and soothing properties. The entire plant can be used.

Rosemary, a cultivated shrub, is an antiseptic and stimulant for the skin. It decongests surface tissue and helps heal the skin.

Sage, a perennial plant found in the Mediterranean area, is an astringent and antiseptic. It is healing and is effective in reducing perspiration. The leaves are the parts of the plant used medicinally. Sage and rosemary are common kitchen spices.

St. John's wort, a perennial shrub native to the east and west coasts of the United States, is an astringent and antiseptic with healing properties. It is useful on irritated or injured skin. The entire plant is used.

Wild Oregon grape is an evergreen shrub found in lower mountainous areas of the Pacific Northwest. The roots are effective as a blood purifier and, as such, can be effective with a number of skin conditions, including acne, eczema and psoriasis.

Witch hazel, a shrub that grows in wooded areas in Canada and the eastern part of the United States, is one of the best known herbs used in skin care. The leaves and bark are astringent and antiseptic and have healing properties.

Yarrow, also known as milfoil, is a perennial plant found throughout the world. It is astringent and drying and stimulates the circulation, thus is used to help improve the functioning of the skin tissue.

ESSENTIAL OILS

Aromatherapy is akin to herbal therapy in that it is a branch of plant medicine. Like herbal therapy, aromatherapy is based on the use of plant materials. Rather than using the various parts of the plant, however, aromatherapy uses the essential oils derived from those plants. Aromatherapy is easier to practice than herbal therapy, because the essential oils are concentrated and penetrate the skin. As with herbs, essential oils should be used only externally.

An essential oil is a phytohormone, or plant hormone, and serves the same function in the plant that animal hormones serve in the human body. In the plant, the essential oil functions as a bactericide, assists in photosynthesis, is the agent that repels pests, and assists in cross-pollenization. The characteristic smell of the plant comes from the essential oils it contains. The purpose of the odor is to attract insects that carry pollen from other plants. Once the plant is pollenated, it stops emitting the scent because it no longer needs to attract insects. The essential oils are then reabsorbed into the plant to serve other purposes.

Essential oils are soluble in fats or alcohols. They are highly volatile and aromatic. Oils are obtained from the plant in a number of ways. The most common method is steam distillation, in which the plant is steamed to separate the oil from the rest of the plant. Oils may also be extracted with solvents or they may be pressed out of the plant by applying pressure. Because essential oils are soluble in fats, two methods of extraction with fat are used. These are enfleurage, in which the plant is placed on beds of fat, where the oils are absorbed, and maceration, in which the plants are bathed in hot fat.

Essential oils have four basic properties that make them important in skin care:

1. They are germicidal.
2. They stimulate or calm.
3. They penetrate.
4. They contain phytohormones.

Four basic properties of essential oils make them useful for skin care—germicidal, stimulatory, penetrating, and phytohormonal.

Essential oils contain aldehydes, esters and phenols. They are natural antiseptics, germicides, and fungicides. All essential oils, regardless of their other characteristics, have this ability to kill bacteria and fungi. In many cases, they are more effective than man-made chemical antiseptics, yet, unlike the chemical substances, are generally harmless to human tissue.

Approximately 20% of all essential oils are soothing. These oils cause the blood vessels to constrict, thus slowing the flow of blood and oxygen.

About 80% of all essential oils are stimulating; they cause the blood vessels to expand, thus increasing the flow of blood and oxygen. Because of their effect on the circulatory system, essential oils are helpful in correcting skin problems associated with poor circulation.

Essential oils also have the ability to penetrate the skin and be absorbed throughout the body. Thus, for example, an aromatherapy massage affects not only the skin, but also the organs beneath the skin in the areas in which the oils are placed. The essential oils can also act as carriers for other molecules designed to penetrate the skin.

The phytohormones contained in the essential oils supplement the natural hormones in the body, helping them work more effectively.

Just as there are many herbs of use in skin care, so are there many essential oils of value. Table 8-2 lists a number of essential oils commonly used in skin care preparations. Many essential oils work best in combination, so that synergy becomes a factor. Essential oils may be purchased individually or in premixed combinations designed for use on various types of skin. Among the essential oils of value in skin care are:

Basil oil is greenish yellow in color and contains the active ingredient linalol. It is a general antiseptic and, like all essential oils, has disinfectant properties. It stimulates the skin and helps decongest pores.

Benzoin, from the gum of an east Indian tree, is reddish brown in color and contains benzoic acid as its active ingredient. Benzoin soothes the skin and helps promote healing for red, dry, or itching skin.

Cajuput oil, from a tree common to the Philippines and Malaysia, contains cineol and terpineol. It is a general antiseptic and healing agent and helps calm the skin. It is useful against acne and psoriasis.

Chamomile oil, blue to greenish blue in color, contains azulene as its principal active ingredient. Chamomile oil soothes the skin and helps promote healing. It is an excellent anti-inflammatory agent and is useful on sensitive skin.

Eucalyptus oil, a clear liquid, contains eucalyptol and tannin as its principal active ingredients. It is an effective bactericide and parasiticide and helps disinfect sores and wounds.

TABLE 8-2

Commonly Used Essential Oils

Oil	Properties	Remarks
Basil oil	antiseptic, stimulating, decongesting	
Benzoin	soothing, healing	useful on red, dry, itching skin
Cajuput	antiseptic, soothing, healing	useful for acne and psoriasis
Chamomile	soothing, healing, anti-inflammatory	useful with sensitive skin
Eucalyptus	antiseptic, germicide	
Geranium	soothing, healing, anti-inflammatory, decongestant	useful on sores, burns, and dry eczema
Hyssop	healing	useful with eczema
Juniper	antiseptic, healing stimulating	useful for acne, weeping eczema, and psoriasis
Lavender	soothing, healing anti-inflammatory	useful for acne, eczema, and psoriasis
Neroli	soothing, healing	
Rosemary	healing, germicide	useful for sores and burns
Sandalwood	soothing, healing anti-inflammatory	
Ylang-ylang	soothing, antiseptic	

Geranium oil, a clear to light green essence, contains terpenes and linalol as its active ingredients. It is an anti-inflammatory agent and soothes and helps heal the skin. It is useful against sores and burns and is effective against dry eczema. Geranium oil can be used with any type of skin but is especially good on congested, oily skin.

Hyssop oil, a light yellow essence, contains borneol and cetone. It is a healing agent and is useful for various skin disorders, including eczema.

Juniper oil, light greenish yellow in color, contains borneol and terpineol. It is an effective antiseptic and healing agent, and stimulates the circulation. Juniper oil is useful against acne, weeping eczema, and psoriasis. It is also good for cleansing and toning oily skin.

Lavender oil, a clear liquid containing linalol and geraniol among its principal active ingredients, is one of the most useful essences. Lavender oil is a soothing and healing agent and has anti-inflammatory properties. It is useful for many skin disorders, including acne, eczema, and psoriasis. This essence is also effective in promoting cell regeneration and is often used in skin-rejuvenating agents. It may be used effectively on all skin types.

Neroli oil, also known as orange blossom oil, is a pale yellow liquid extracted from Seville orange flowers. Its principal active ingredients are linalol and geraniol. It has soothing and healing properties and is useful on all types of skin. Like lavender oil, neroli helps cell regeneration.

Rosemary oil, a clear liquid, contains pinene and cineol among its ingredients. It is a healing agent and parasiticide. It is useful as an astringent and toner for the skin, and is effective against burns and sores.

Sandalwood oil, a thick greenish-yellow liquid, contains terpenes. This oil is one of the most useful essences for skin care and may be used on all skin types. It is an antiseptic and healing agent and is effective in relieving itching and inflammation. It also acts as an astringent.

Ylang-ylang oil, a light yellow liquid, contains geraniol, linalol, and salicylic acid. It is antiseptic and soothing to the skin. Although it can be used with any skin type, it is especially effective on oily skin.

SEA WATER AND SEA PRODUCTS

The use of sea water and sea products has a valuable place in skin care. Marine clays, algaes, and sea plants, as well as sea water itself can be used effectively to cleanse and revitalize skin tissue.

All life came from the sea. The composition of sea water is identical to the composition of the natural fluids of the body. Sea water contains, in the same proportions, all of the trace elements, vitamins, amino acids, and minerals that are necessary to sustain life. Table 8-3 shows the composition of sea water.

TABLE 8-3

Composition of Sea Water

Element	Amount (g/L)
Chlorine	19.00
Sodium	10.50
Magnesium	1.35
Sulfur	0.89
Calcium	0.40
Potassium	0.38
Bromine	0.07
Carbon	0.03
Strontium	0.008
Boron	0.005
Silicon	0.003
Fluorine	0.001

The human body contains 60% to 85% water, depending on age. Children's bodies contain up to 85% water; older peoples' bodies, down to 60%, as aging is partly a process of drying out. The body fluids consist of blood (about 5%), lymph (about 15%), intercellular fluid (about 25%), and interstitial fluid (about 25%). All cells continually bathe in water. This water closely resembles sea water.

The water bathing a body's cells closely resembles sea water.

The products of the sea—seaweed, algae, and sediments—also have beneficial properties, and are generally more readily available than sea water. Seaweed and algae accumulate and concentrate all of the materials contained in the ocean. One kilogram of seaweed (2.2 lb) contains the same mineral wealth as 10,000 liters (2,500 gallons) of sea water. Sediments, such as peloids, a blend of mud and oyster secretions, and clays, also contain many trace elements and minerals.

The marine plants, as used in skin care, perform a number of vital functions. They remineralize and rehydrate the skin, helping to retain moisture. They contain phytohormones, which are compatible with human hormones, and thus, work in the same manner as essential oils and herbs. They are rich sources of iodine, which acts on the thyroid gland, helping it secrete more thyroxine, important to the body's immune system. Seaweed is helpful in treating acne. Because of its iodine content, however, seaweed should not be used by people who are allergic to shellfish or are acne prone.

Seaweed and algae stimulate circulation, thus aiding nutrition and detoxification of the cells. Clays and peloids, on the other hand, have a soothing and calming effect and help decongest pores. Sea products work especially well when used in conjunction with essential oils. Seaweeds and algae are also excellent dietary supplements.

In algae pack treatments, algae is mixed with sea water to make a thick paste. The paste is spread along the person's spine and covered with paraffin. He or she then lies under heat lamps for 30 to 45 minutes. The spinal column is chosen as the site of the treatment because the spine contains the bones closest to the surface of the body and major arteries and veins pass along the column. The marine ions diffuse quickly and penetrate more rapidly into the body from this area.

Chapter 9

The Importance
of Nutrition

The body relies on an adequate intake of quality nutrients to function properly. The skin is no exception. When nutrients are of good quality and are taken in sufficient quantities and in the proper balance, the skin is healthy. It will have good color and vitality, adequate moisture and sebum production, and will function normally. When some or all of the required nutrients are missing from the diet, the skin may appear dull and lifeless, with poor color and improper functioning. Only the nervous system consumes more nutrients than the skin. When the body is short of nutrients, preference goes to the nervous system, so the skin goes hungry.

Poor nutrition directly affects the health of the skin. It indirectly affects the skin. When other organs in the body malfunction, symptoms often manifest themselves in the skin. So, it is difficult to separate the effects of nutrition on the skin from its effects on the rest of the body.

It is important to understand the principles of nutrition and diet and how they affect the skin. Knowing how the various nutrients work, what they do and what happens when they are deficient, can help reach the root causes of skin problems.

THE NUTRITIONAL PROCESS

Think of the body as a factory. Like a manufacturing plant, raw materials are taken in, products are manufactured, and waste materials are thrown away. In the case of the body, the raw materials are the nutrients that come from food, water, and air. The food and water are ingested and pass through the digestive system; the air comes in through the lungs. The products manufactured are energy and tissue, resulting from the complex chemical process called metabolism. The waste products, carbon dioxide, feces, and urine, are eliminated through the excretory system. Like the manufacturing plant, the quality of the products is only as good as the raw materials that go into making them.

The nutritional process has three parts. The first is ingestion, the second is digestion, and the third is elimination. All three work together equally to fuel the body and keep it healthy. This relationship is illustrated in Figure 9-1.

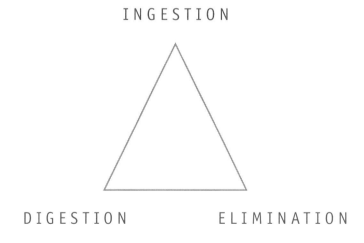

Figure 9-1
The nutritional process

Black Skin Care for the Practicing Professional

In the first part, *ingestion,* food is chosen, prepared, and taken into the body. Good nutrition starts with the choice of food. Today, there is an almost infinite variety of foods from which to choose. Good foods contain the necessary nutrients to fuel the body. Foods that are poor in nutrients, offer only empty calories. The better the food that is ingested, the better the nutritional process.

Preparation is also important. Good foods, improperly prepared, can lose much of their nutritive value. Overuse of pesticides, additives, and preservatives can lower the quality of the food, as can overcooking.

Digestion, the second part of the nutritional process, begins when the food is placed in the mouth. As the food is chewed, it is broken into smaller pieces that are easier to digest. Saliva, the first enzyme encountered in the digestive process, is secreted by the salivary glands in the mouth. These enzymes, proteins that act as catalysts to change other substances while retaining their own identity, start the breakdown of the food into a useable form.

After swallowing, the food travels down the esophagus to the stomach where gastric juices consisting of hydrochloric acid and other enzymes continue the breakdown of the food. The food becomes a liquid, called chyme. From the stomach, the chyme moves into the small intestine. The pancreas and the liver produce more enzymes that break the food down even further.

The nutrients digested from the food, in the form of glucose, amino acids, and fatty acids, are absorbed into the bloodstream and lymphatic system through the walls of the small intestine. From here, they are transported to the various organs where they are converted into energy or tissue by the process of metabolism.

The undigested portion of the food passes from the small intestine to the large intestine, where the third part of the nutritional process, *elimination,* starts. The waste products are then expelled from the body in the form of feces and urine.

Proper elimination is just as vital to the health of the skin as the other two parts of the process. The body has to rid itself of waste materials before they putrefy and spread toxins throughout the body.

The process by which the nutrients are converted into tissue or energy is called *metabolism*. There are two phases—anabolism, the chemical conversion of nutrients to build up tissue and body chemicals, and catabolism, the breakdown of nutrients to supply energy. Both phases occur simultaneously.

NUTRIENTS

Nutrients are the carbohydrates, proteins, fats, vitamins, minerals, and water contained in the food. Each type of nutrient performs a different function for the body, either providing fuel for energy, for building tissue, or for helping to regulate the processes of the body. The fuel value of a given nutrient is expressed in calories, a measure of the amount of heat produced when the nutrient is oxidized. Thus, high-calorie foods have more potential for producing energy than low-calorie foods.

Nutrients in our food provide fuel for creating energy, for building tissues, or for regulating the body's processes.

Carbohydrates

Carbohydrates supply most of the body's energy needs, whether for the production of heat, to keep the body temperature constant; for mechanical energy, to enable the muscles to work; or for electrical energy, to allow the nervous system to work.

The principal carbohydrates are sugar, starch and cellulose. Through the action of enzymes, the simple carbohydrate, sugar, and the complex carbohydrate, starch, are converted into glucose. The glucose is either used immediately for energy or is further converted into glycogen and stored in the liver or in muscle tissue. The rest is converted into fat and stored throughout the body for later use. Cellulose is not digestible, so is not useful for energy conversion.

Protein

Protein provides the materials for building tissue and for the production of hormones and enzymes. When carbohydrates and fat are deficient, the metabolism burns protein as a source of energy. Like excess carbohydrate, excess protein is converted into fat and stored in body tissue. The first areas to be affected by protein deficiency are the skin, hair, and nails.

Amino acids, the building blocks of the body, are produced by the action of digestion of the proteins. The body needs 22 different amino acids. However, the body is capable of producing only 14 of them. The other eight, called the essential amino acids, must come from food. All eight of these must be present in specific proportions for synthesis to occur. Because animal products (e.g., meat) generally contain all eight essential amino acids, they are called complete proteins. Fruits and vegetables are incomplete proteins because they generally lack one or more of these eight. So care must be taken to combine these foods to get the proper mix of the essential amino acids. Table 9-1 lists the amino acids.

Fats

Fats provide a concentrated source of energy. When fats are oxidized, they give up twice as many calories as carbohydrates and proteins. They also carry the fat-soluble vitamins. They are the slowest of the main nutrients to be digested.

Animal fats are saturated, that is, they cannot accept any more hydrogen atoms in their structural chain, and tend to be solid at room temperature. Vegetable fats are unsaturated, that is, they can accept more hydrogen atoms, and tend to be liquid at room temperature. Vegetable oils, however, can be hydrogenated by adding gaseous hydrogen under pressure to convert the oil into solid form.

Fatty acids give fats their characteristic taste and texture. During digestion, the fatty acids are split from the structural chain and pass through the intestinal wall into the bloodstream. Three of the fatty acids—linoleic, arachidonic, and linolenic—are collectively known as vitamin F and are discussed in more detail in the section on vitamins.

Vitamins

Vitamins, certain organic substances found in food, are essential to life and health, even though they do not provide energy or build tissue like the three major nutrients. Vitamins are catalysts that help manufacture

TABLE 9-1

Amino Acids

Amino Acid	Formula
Alanine	$H_7NC_3O_2$
Arginine	$H_{14}N_4C_6O_2$
Asparagine	$H_8N_2C_4O_3$
Aspartic acid	$H_7NC_4O_4$
Cystine	$H_{11}N_2S_2C_6O_4$
Glutamic acid	$H_9NC_5O_4$
Glutamine	$H_{10}N_2C_5O_3$
Glycine	$H_5NC_2O_2$
Histidine	$H_9N_3C_5O_3$
Hydroxylysine	$H_{14}N_2C_6O_3$
Hydroxyproline	$H_{10}NC_5O_3$
Isoleucine[*]	$H_{13}NC_6O_2$[†]
Leucine[*]	$H_{13}NC_6O_2$[†]
Lysine[*]	$H_{14}N_2C_6O_2$
Methionine[*]	$H_{11}NSC_5O_2$
Phenylalanine[*]	$H_6NC_9O_2$
Proline	$H_{10}NC_5O_2$
Serine	$H_7NC_3O_3$
Threonine[*]	$H_9NC_4O_3$
Tryptophan[*]	$H_8N_2C_{11}O_2$
Tyrosine	$H_7NC_9O_3$
Valine[*]	$H_{11}NC_5O_2$

[*] Essential amino acids
[†] Isoleucine and leucine have the same chemical formula but differ structurally.

enzymes and regulate the metabolism so the carbohydrates, proteins, and fats can do their work. Because the body can form very few of the vitamins on its own, they must be supplied through the diet. There are at least 20 vitamins known at present. Some are water soluble; others are fat soluble. Table 9-2 lists the vitamins.

Most vitamins must be supplied through the diet because the body can form very few on its own.

TABLE 9-2

Vitamins

Vitamin	Common name	Source	Remarks
A		green leafy vegetables, carrots, fish-liver oil, butter, cream	important for skin; RDA— 5,000 IU; toxic in large doses
B *complex*			
B_1	thiamine	wheat germ, bran, brewer's yeast	important for skin
B_2	riboflavin	wheat germ, bran, brewer's yeast	important for skin
B_3	niacin	poultry, fish, peanuts, lean meat	important for skin
B_5	pantothenic acid	organ meats, egg yolks, whole grains	
B_6	pyridoxine	meat, whole grains	
B_{12}	cobalamin	organ meats, fish, dairy products	
B_{13}	orotic acid	whey, root vegetables	

continued on next page

B_{15}	pangamic acid	whole grains, seeds, brown rice	
Biotin		organ meats, egg yolks	also known as vitamin H
Choline		wheat germ, liver, egg yolk	
Inositol		whole grains, liver, citrus fruit	important for hair growth
Folic acid		liver, leafy green vegetables	also known as vitamin M
PABA		liver, wheat germ, yeast	important for skin; sunscreen
C	ascorbic acid	fruits, vegetables	important for skin; RDA—60 mg
D		fish-liver oils.	RDA—400 IU
E	tocopherol	wheat germ oil, seeds, nuts, soybeans	important for skin; RDA—5–15 IU
F	fatty acids	vegetable oils, cod-liver oil	
K	menadione	kelp, leafy green vegetables	synthesized in body
P	bioflavonoids	citrus fruit, grapes, cherries	important for skin
T		egg yolk, sesame seeds	
U		raw cabbage	

- Vitamin A, a fat-soluble vitamin, is found as preformed vitamin A in fish-liver oil, cream, and butter. It is found as carotene in green leafy vegetables and carrots. The body converts carotene to vitamin A for use. This vitamin is necessary for proper growth of the bottom layer of skin and is used in the treatment of acne. The Recommended Dietary Allowance (RDA) for vitamin A is 5,000 international units (IU) for adults. Vitamin A can be toxic in extremely high doses.

- Vitamin B complex, a group of water-soluble vitamins, are found in bacteria, yeasts, and molds. These vitamins are necessary for the conversion of carbohydrates to glucose, which is burned to provide the body with energy. They are also necessary for proper metabolism and for the nervous system. All of the members of this group are interrelated in their function and should be taken together. Brewer's yeast and green vegetables are good sources of the B complex vitamins.

- Vitamin B_1 (thiamine) is needed for the conversion of carbohydrates to glucose and is found in wheat germ and bran. Thiamine is synthesized in the body by the intestinal flora.

- Vitamin B_2 (riboflavin) is vital to cell respiration and is important to healthy skin. It is found in the same foods that contain the other B complex vitamins. Riboflavin may also be synthesized by the intestinal flora.

- Vitamin B_3 (niacin) is necessary for healthy skin and as a coenzyme for breaking down the major nutrients. It is found in lean meats, poultry, fish, and peanuts. The body also converts the amino acid, tryptophan, into niacin.

- Vitamin B_5 (pantothenic acid) is needed for healthy skin and is important in cellular metabolism. It also helps retard aging and wrinkling. It is found in organ meats, egg yolks, and whole grains. Pantothenic acid is also synthesized by the intestinal flora.

- Vitamin B_6 (pyridoxine) aids in the production of hydrochloric acid and helps linoleic acid, one of the essential fatty acids, work better. It is also needed for the synthesis of DNA and RNA. This vitamin is found in meat and whole grains.

- Vitamin B_{12} (cobalamin) contains mineral elements and is needed for proper metabolism. It is found in organ meats, fish, and dairy products. Unlike other vitamins, vitamin B_{12} cannot be produced synthetically. Vitamin B_{12} is also injectable.

- Vitamin B_{13} (orotic acid) helps in cellular restoration and is used in the production of folic acid and vitamin B_{12}. It is found in whey and in root vegetables.

- Vitamin B_{15} (pangamic acid) helps cell respiration and is needed for the metabolism of protein. It is found in whole grains, seeds, and brown rice.

- Biotin, sometimes called vitamin H, is a coenzyme that aids the production of fatty acids and is essential for proper nutrition. It is found in organ meats and egg yolks.

- Choline is necessary for a healthy liver and kidneys and for the absorption of fat by the body. It is found in lecithin, liver, wheat germ, and egg yolk.

- Inositol works with choline in the metabolism of fat. It is also important to hair growth. Inositol is found in lecithin, whole grains, liver, and citrus fruits.

- Folic acid, sometimes called vitamin M, helps in the formation of red blood cells and in the formation of nucleic acid. It also helps the liver function properly. Folic acid is found in liver and in green leafy vegetables.

- Para-aminobenzoic acid (PABA) helps the intestinal flora produce folic acid and is important to the health of the skin. PABA is also effective as a sunscreen. It is found in liver, wheat germ, and yeast.

- Vitamin C (ascorbic acid) is a water-soluble vitamin. It is less stable than the other vitamins and is oxidized easily. It is found in most fruits and vegetables, especially in citrus fruits. Vitamin C is important to the maintenance of collagen and the formation of connective tissue. It also helps many of the other nutrients function properly. In addition, vitamin C helps combat stress and acts as a natural antibiotic. Unlike some other vitamins, humans cannot synthesize vitamin C, so the entire requirement for this vitamin must be supplied through the diet.

  Vitamin C cannot be synthesized by the body so the RDA must be supplied by the diet.

  The RDA for vitamin C is 60 mg, although smokers may need additional quantities of this nutrient, because smoking destroys vitamin C. There is no toxicity from excessive intake of vitamin C, although some people may experience some side effects, such as diarrhea or a rash.

- Vitamin D, the "sunshine vitamin," is fat soluble. It is synthesized in the body through the action of sunlight on the skin, and is also present in fish-liver oils. Vitamin D aids normal growth and bone formation and helps maintain stability in the central nervous system. The RDA for vitamin D is 400 IU. Extremely large doses of vitamin D can be toxic. Milk is generally fortified with synthetic vitamin D.

- Vitamin E (tocopherol) is fat soluble. It is found in wheat germ oil, whole raw seeds, nuts, and soybeans. Vitamin E is an antioxidant and helps prevent the breakdown of fatty acids and other vitamins and the formation of free radicals. This nutrient is also important to cellular respiration and helps increase stamina and endurance. It also helps prevent the formation of scars on the skin. The RDA for vitamin E varies from 5 IU for infants to 15 IU for adults. Although vitamin E is generally not toxic, it may be harmful to persons with high blood pressure. Vitamin E is also used as an ingredient in some topical skin care products.

- Vitamin F, which consists of the three unsaturated fatty acids, linoleic, linolenic, and arachidonic, is necessary for normal functioning of the glands and for the regulation of blood coagulation. The unsaturated fatty acids also lubricate cells and nourish skin cells. Linoleic acid is an essential fatty acid, that is, it cannot be synthesized by the body and must be supplied in the diet. The other two can be synthesized from linoleic acid.

  Although there is no RDA established for unsaturated fatty acids, it is generally recommended that linoleic acid make up about 1% of the daily caloric intake. Vitamin F is not toxic, but excessive consumption of fatty acids can result in weight gain. Food sources for unsaturated fatty acids include natural vegetable oils, cod-liver oil, and wheat germ.

- Vitamin K (menadione) is fat soluble and is manufactured in the body by intestinal flora. It is also found in kelp and leafy green vegetables. Vitamin K is important for proper liver function and for the formation of some of the chemicals required for various body processes. It also helps foster proper blood clotting. Natural vitamin K is not toxic although excessive doses of synthetic vitamin K can produce toxic symptoms. Because it is synthesized by the body, deficiencies are rare, so no RDA has been established. Other sources of vitamin K are yogurt, alfalfa, and fish-liver oils.

- Vitamin P (bioflavonoids) consists of a water-soluble group of nutrients that occur with vitamin C in many fruits and vegetables. These nutrients, which consist of rutin, hesperidin, citrin, flavone, and flavonals, are needed to allow vitamin C to be used effectively. They also help in the formation of collagen and strengthen capillary walls. No RDA has been established for the bioflavonoids and they are considered to be nontoxic. Food sources include citrus fruits, buckwheat, rose hips, grapes, and cherries.

- Vitamin T and vitamin U are little known and their use is not yet fully understood. Vitamin T assists in the blood coagulation process and is found in egg yolks and sesame seeds. Vitamin U, found in raw cabbage, helps heal ulcers. Because so little is known about these two vitamins, no RDA has been established for either of them.

Minerals

Like vitamins, minerals are essential to proper body functioning. Minerals are inorganic nutrients that let vitamins work. Without them, vitamins would be unable to function. All of the minerals needed by the body must be supplied in the diet. None can be synthesized by the body. In their pure mineral form, these substances are largely indigestible. Before the body can use them, they must be made digestible through the process of chelation, in which the mineral bonds with an amino acid. Table 9-3 lists the various minerals.

At present, 18 minerals are known to be important to life. The most important—calcium, iodine, iron, magnesium, phosphorus and zinc—have had RDAs established. The other 12 minerals—chlorine, chromium, cobalt, copper, fluorine, manganese, molybdenum, potassium, selenium, sodium, sulfur, and vanadium—though also important, have not had RDAs set.

Minerals are essential to proper body functioning and let vitamins work.

- Calcium is the most abundant material in the body. It operates in conjunction with phosphorus to form bones and teeth. It also helps maintain healthy skin and helps prevent sun damage to the skin. Sources of calcium are milk, dairy products, soybeans, salmon, and bone meal. The RDA for calcium varies from 800 to 1200 mg.

TABLE 9-3

Minerals

Mineral	Source	Remarks
Calcium	bone meal, milk, soybeans, salmon	important to skin, RDA—800–1200 mg
Chlorine	salt	
Chromium	eggs, liver, mushrooms, brewer's yeast	
Cobalt	meat, sea vegetables, milk, shellfish	
Copper	seafood, liver, whole grains, legumes, leafy green vegetables	important to skin
Fluorine	seafood, cheese, fluoridated water	
Iodine	fish, sea vegetables	RDA—1 µg/ kg of body weight
Iron	organ meats, whole grains, leafy green vegetables	RDA—10–18 mg
Magnesium	green vegetables, whole grains, soybeans	RDA—300–350 mg
Manganese	whole grains, nuts, green vegetables, eggs	
Molybdenum	meats, cereals, dark green leafy vegetables	
Phosphorus	meat, poultry, fish, eggs, whole grains	RDA—800 mg

continued

Potassium	leafy green vegetables bananas, potatoes	important to skin
Selenium	organ meats, fish, brewer's yeast	important to skin
Sodium	salt	
Sulfur	eggs, meat, fish	important to skin
Vanadium	organ meats, seafood	
Zinc	meats, eggs, wheatgerm	important to skin

- Chlorine is generally found combined with sodium or potassium in the form of sodium or potassium chloride, or salt. Chlorine is needed to regulate the acid-alkali balance of the blood and to help maintain intercellular pressure. Most chlorine is supplied through the ingestion of salt in the diet. Chlorine deficiency may lead to hair loss.

- Chromium is essential for the proper enzymatic action in metabolism and for regulating blood sugar levels. It is needed in small concentrations. Food sources include eggs, liver, mushrooms, and brewer's yeast.

- Cobalt, a component of vitamin B_{12}, is necessary for proper cellular functioning. Meat, especially organ meats, sea vegetables, shellfish, and milk are food sources for cobalt.

- Copper is important to the skin, nerves, and blood. It helps the amino acid, tyrosine, function to pigment the skin and works with vitamin C to form elastin. In addition, it helps form the myelin sheaths around nerve fibers and assists the development of hemoglobin in the blood. Copper is found in seafood, liver, whole grains, legumes, and leafy green vegetables. Copper deficiency may inhibit healing of skin sores.

- Fluorine helps strengthen bones and teeth. Although needed in small quantities for good health, fluorine is toxic in high concentration. In the United States, most fluorine is supplied in fluoridated water. Food sources include seafood and cheese.

- Iodine is necessary for the proper functioning of the thyroid gland. This mineral helps regulate energy, control the metabolism, and influence growth and development. The RDA for iodine is about 1μg/kg of body weight. Pregnant women should ingest slightly higher amounts. The best food sources for iodine are fish and sea vegetables. Iodine deficiency may lead to dry hair.

- Iron is important to the quality of the blood. This mineral combines with copper to help produce hemoglobin, which carries the oxygen in the blood. In addition, iron helps form myoglobin in muscle tissue. The RDA for iron is between 10 and 18 mg. Women require more iron than men. Organ meats, whole grains, and leafy green vegetables are the best dietary sources of iron.

- Magnesium is essential to metabolism and the maintenance of a suitable acid-alkali balance. It also helps convert blood sugar into energy. The RDA for magnesium varies from 300 to 350 mg, the lower amount for men, the higher amount for women. This mineral is found in most foods, especially in green vegetables, soybeans, whole grains, and apples.

- Manganese helps activate a number of enzymes that promote the functioning of vitamins. It also helps feed nerves and brain tissue. Food sources of manganese include whole grains, nuts, green vegetables, and eggs.

- Molybdenum helps iron and copper function properly in the body. Meats, cereals, and dark green leafy vegetables are good food sources for this mineral.

- Phosphorus is second only to calcium in its presence in the body. Like calcium, phosphorus is necessary to proper growth and healthy bones and teeth. For best functioning, these two minerals should be combined in specific proportions. The RDA for phosphorus is 800 mg. All high-protein foods contain phosphorus. These include meat, poultry, fish, eggs, and whole grains.

- Potassium works with sodium to help regulate the balance between intercellular and intracellular fluid. These two minerals also help equalize the acid-alkali balance and are important for muscle functioning. Potassium also helps promote healthy skin. Potassium is found in green leafy vegetables, bananas, potatoes, and whole grains.

- Selenium is necessary to maintain elasticity in tissues and for reproduction. An antioxidant, selenium works with vitamin E to help retard aging. Organ meats, fish, brewer's yeast, and whole grains are food sources for this mineral.

- Sodium, in addition to working with potassium, helps maintain the solubility of other minerals in the blood. It also helps produce hydrochloric acid in the stomach. Present in most foods, sodium is one of the few nutrients for which there is little chance of deficiency. Table salt is the principle source of sodium in the diet.

- Sulfur, a component of keratin, is essential for healthy skin and hair. It also helps in tissue respiration. Eggs, meat, fish, and dairy products are good food sources for sulfur. Sulfur is necessary for a good complexion. It keeps the skin smooth and youthful and it keeps hair glossy and smooth.

- Vanadium helps in the proper development of bones and teeth. It also helps iron function in blood formation. Food sources of vanadium include organ meats, seafood, and whole grains.

- Zinc is important for the proper functioning of many vitamins and enzymes as well as for normal growth and development. It also assists the body's natural healing processes. Zinc is essential for healthy skin. The RDA for this mineral is 15 mg. Food sources include meats, eggs, wheat germ, and brewer's yeast.

Water

Water is probably the most important nutrient of all. A person can survive for weeks without food, but only for days without water. It comprises almost two thirds of the body's weight and is a part of virtually every bodily process from digestion through elimination. Water carries the other nutrients through the body and carries the waste products from the body. It also helps regulate body temperature. The amount of water the body needs daily varies according to how much is lost due to activity and environmental conditions.

Water needs increase during exercise, in hot weather, and for the elderly. During exercise or in hot weather water is lost through perspiration and respiration. This water must be replenished to prevent heat exhaustion or heat stroke.

The body's need for water is absolute, but the amount required varies with a person's activity and the environmental conditions.

Heat exhaustion results from high temperatures during exercise. It can also occur while a person is at leisure. It is also common among the elderly who take diuretics prescribed by their physicians. The symptoms of heat exhaustion include weakness, vertigo, nausea, and vomiting. Faintness may precede collapse. The person may have a gray color. The skin is usually cold and clammy. Onset is sudden, but the duration is brief. Treatment for heat exhaustion consists of placing the person in a cool environment and giving fluids by mouth. Intravenous fluids are seldom necessary.

Heat stroke is a serious condition that, if left untreated, can be fatal. It is common among the elderly who suffer from preexisting chronic diseases or who are using diuretics. Military recruits and athletes who are exposed to high temperatures during vigorous exercise, and who lose large volumes of water as a result, are also at risk of heat stroke. The symptoms of heat stroke include high body temperatures (greater than 106° F.), and the inability to sweat. The skin is hot and dry, the pulse is racing, respiration is rapid and shallow, and the blood pressure is low. Treatment must be immediate. The person should be placed in a cool environment. Clothing should be removed and he or she should be immersed in an ice bath. The skin should be gently massaged. Fluids should be administered orally and intravenously.

Nutritionists advise drinking 6 to 8 glasses of water daily. Tea, coffee, and alcohol do not count. These beverages act as diuretics and promote water loss. One ounce of alcohol, for example, uses 8 ounces of water for digestion.

Water lost during exercise must be replaced. Twelve to 16 ounces of water are required to make up for every 2 pounds lost while exercising.

Urine color is a good indication of the body's need for water replenishment. The urine should be pale yellow in color. If it is dark, the body needs more water, so water intake should be increased.

Sports drinks are currently popular. They are necessary for people who lose large volumes of water during exercise or work. These drinks contain sodium, which lets the body retain more water. Plain water does not contain sodium, so more plain water is required to replenish lost water.

A typical sports drink contains 50 to 100 mg of sodium per serving. The daily adult bodily requirement for sodium is 1100 to 3300 mg. For most Americans, the daily sodium intake is 10 to 60 times that necessary for good health. As a result, most people will not benefit from sports drinks because their daily sodium load is more than adequate.

GUIDELINES TO GOOD NUTRITION

Good nutritional habits are a vital part of the overall skin care regime. The U. S. Department of Health and Human Services has published a list of seven dietary guidelines that can serve as a model for this advice (*Nutrition and Your Health: Dietary Guidelines for Americans*).

Follow the seven guidelines for good nutrition!

1. Eat a Variety of Foods. Although most foods contain more than one of the nutrients needed for good health, no one food contains them all. The only way to ensure an adequate intake of nutrients is to eat a balanced diet that contains foods from the following groups: fruits and vegetables; cereals, whole grains, and grain products; dairy products, such as milk, cheese, and yogurt; meats, poultry, fish and eggs; and legumes, such as beans and peas.

With a balanced diet, there will be little need for taking extra vitamins or food supplements, although some people, notably pregnant women, the elderly, or women of child-bearing age, may need additional nutrients.

Men's nutritional needs differ from those of women. Men need about 2,300 to 2,700 calories per day, while women require only 1,600 to 2,400. In addition, women need food that is richer in nutrients.

2. Maintain an Ideal Weight. Everyone has an ideal weight, at which all the body systems operate most efficiently and at which health is optimized. This weight is based on height, build, and metabolism. Significant deviation from this ideal weight can lead to a variety of disorders.

Obesity increases the risk of high blood pressure, high triglyceride levels, increased cholesterol, diabetes, and higher risk of heart attack and of strokes.

A program for weight loss, to have the best chance for success in the long term, can only be based on reducing the caloric intake and increasing the amount of exercise. Weight loss should be gradual, no more than 1 to 2 pounds per week. Unfortunately, there are no quick and easy ways to lose weight permanently. It takes an adjustment of dietary habits.

3. Avoid Too Much Fat, Saturated Fat, and Cholesterol. A high blood cholesterol level increases the risk of heart attack. Diets rich in fats and saturated fats tend to increase blood cholesterol levels in most people. To control the cholesterol level, it is wise to limit the intake of foods high in fats. Fat intake should be limited to about 30% of the calorie total.

Good low-cholesterol protein sources include lean meat, fish, poultry, dry beans, and peas. Organ meats and eggs are high in cholesterol but contain many vitamins, minerals, and other important nutrients, so should be eaten in moderation.

Butter, cream, and most shortenings are high in cholesterol, so their intake should be limited. Foods should be prepared by boiling, baking, or broiling, rather than by frying.

4. Eat Foods with Adequate Starch and Fiber. The energy the body needs is supplied by both carbohydrates and fats. If fat intake is limited, the intake of carbohydrates should be increased to maintain the required caloric level.

In general, a low-fat, high-carbohydrate diet is healthiest. Carbohydrates contain about half as many calories per ounce as fats. In addition, the energy from fats is stored in the stomach and hips where it becomes body fat. The energy from carbohydrates, however, is stored in the muscles and liver.

Complex carbohydrates provide energy along with other vitamins and minerals. They also increase the amount of fiber consumed in the diet. Diets higher in fiber reduce chronic constipation and may help reduce the risk of some forms of cancer.

Whole grain breads, cereals, pasta, fruits and vegetables, beans, peas, and nuts are good sources of starch and fiber.

5. Avoid Too Much Sugar. The average American consumes 130 lb of sugar per year, either through direct use or through sweeteners added to foods or naturally present in foods. The major dietary problem with added sugar is the risk of tooth decay. It is best to limit the use of white and brown sugar, honey, and syrups and to use moderation in the consumption of foods containing these substances.

6. Avoid Too Much Sodium. The body needs sodium to function properly. The amount needed is about 1,000 mg/1,000 calories consumed. One teaspoon of salt equals 3 g. The American diet, however, contains much more sodium than is needed. Most processed foods, many beverages, and many condiments contain large quantities of salt. In addition, many people add table salt to their food.

Excess sodium consumption may lead to high blood pressure, which is a significant health risk. It is best to limit the use of salt to reduce the intake of sodium. Add only small amounts of salt during cooking and do not add salt to the food at the table. Limit the intake of salty foods, especially snack foods such as potato chips and pretzels. Use other herbs and spices for flavoring.

7. Drink Alcohol Only in Moderation. Alcohol has little or no nutritional value but is high in calories. In addition, alcohol alters the rate of absorption of some nutrients, making them less useful to the body. Heavy drinkers may, therefore, suffer from vitamin and mineral deficiencies. In addition, heavy alcohol consumption may lead to diseases such as cirrhosis of the liver and to some types of cancer and may cause birth defects. The high caloric content of alcohol makes it difficult to drink while on a diet.

Alcohol consumed in moderation, 1.5 ounces of pure alcohol—that is, one or two mixed drinks, 8 ounces of wine, or 24 ounces of beer—per day, does not seem to be harmful to adults, however. So, drink only in moderation.

Glossary/Index

Neroli oil, has soothing and healing properties, 194, 195
Nerves, 13, 22–25
Nervous system, balancing, 94
Neutrons, 159
Niacin, 207
Nicotine, 41
Nicotine stains, 41
Night creams, 167
No-lye relaxers, combination products that require mixing two chemicals together to start the relaxing process,121
Normal skin, skin that is in proper balance, 29: masks for, 100
Normalization and treatment, 71, 81–83: and facial masks, 80
Nutrients, 81, 202–217: absorption of, 201; for skin, 13, 71
Nutrition: guidelines for, 218–220; and skin health, 199
Nutrition and Your Health: Dietary Guidelines for Americans, 218
Nutritional process, 200–202
NWS, the National Weather Service, 152–153

0

Occupation, and skin health, 2
Occupational Safety and Health Act, 107
Oil absorbers, 168
Oil dryness, 31, 33
Oily skin, sebaceous glands produce more oil than is necessary for proper skin function, 29–31: and acne, 59; and black skin, 3; and disincrustation, 77; essential oils for treating, 195; foundations for, 142, 143; masks for, 100; pH of, 162; vacuuming, 77; *see also* Combination skin
Ointments, 186
Onychomycosis, a fungal infection of the finger and toenails, 135
Opacifiers, 174
Orange blossom oil, *see* Neroli oil
Organic chemistry, is concerned with compounds that contain carbon, the essential component for all living things, 158
Orotic acid, 208

OSHA, Occupational Safety and Health Act, 107
Overheating, 3
Oxidation-reduction reactions, 162
Oxygen, absorption of, 27
Ozone, 81
Ozone layer, depletion of, 152

P

PABA, Para-aminobenzoic acid, 153, 208–209
Pacinian corpuscles, 22
Packaging of skin care products, 169–170
Pain, 22
Pangamic acid, 208
Panniculus adiposus, *see* Subcutaneous layer
Pantothenic acid, 207
Papillary layer, the thinner of the dermal layers, lying just below the dermis, 12–13
Para-aminobenzoic acid (PABA), 153, 208–209
Paraffin masks, 101–102
Parasiticides, 193, 195
Patch tests, 125, 127
Pattern baldness, 129
Pedicures, 50, 132
Peels, 67, 168
Peloids, 197
Permanent haircoloring, 124–126
Permanent waving, 126–127: and haircoloring, 125
Perspiration, *see* Sweat
Pesticides, 201
Petrissage, kneading, wringing, pulling, and rocking motions used to massage the deeper muscle masses of the limbs and fleshy areas of the body, 95
Petrolatum, 173
Peutz-Jegher syndrome, 45
PH, a logarithmic scale, measured from 0 to 14, that measures the degree of acidity or alkalinity, 65, 162: chart of, 163; and cleansers, 88; controlling, 172; and permanent waving, 127; of skin, 27, 162
Phagocytes, 45
Pharmaceuticals, *see* Drugs
Phenol, 106

Phenols, 192

Pheromones, 18

Phosphorus, 212, 214

Photosensitivity, and acne medication, 65

Physicians: advice of, 185; referring clients to, 45, 106, 131; skin care services of, 70

Physiologic functions of skin, 25–26

Phytohormones, plant hormones, 192

Pigmentation: changes in, 33; uneven, 4

Pilary canal, 20

Pilary system, consists of the hair and the hair follicles, 16

Pinene, 195

Pityriasis alba, 47

Plasticizers, 42

Poison ivy, 42

Pollution, 42: and volatile organic compounds, 164

Polysorbate 80, 173, 174

Pores: clogged, 29, 33, 59; essential oils for decongesting, 193; size of, 29, 31

Porosity, ability of the hair to absorb moisture, 116

Postinflammatory hyperpigmentation (PIH), 45

Postinflammatory hypopigmentation, 47

Posture, 94

Potassium, 213, 214

Poultices, 186

Powders, 143–144

Pregnancy: and keloid scars, 53; and vitiligo, 49

Preservatives, 174, 176, 181, 201

Pressure, is applied to pressure points, or tsubos, along the meridians to remove energy blockages, 96–99

Pressure points, 96, 99

Pressure receptors, *see* Pacinian corpuscles

Prevention, keeping new germs from growing, 105

Prickle cell layer, *see* Stratum spinosum

Product claims, 179–182

Propylene glycol, 174

Propylparaben, 176

Protectants, 172

Protective function of skin, 10, 25, 26

Protein, 202–203

Protons, 159

Pseudofolliculitis barber, an inflammatory condition in which hard coarse shaved hair regrows into the skin, 54–55

Psoralen, 48, 130

Psoriasis, 113: essential oils for treating, 193, 195

Psychological action of skin care products, 177

Pyridoxine, 208

Q

Quaternary ammonium compounds, 106

R

Race: categories of, 2; and hair, 115–116; and skin care, 1

Razor bump, *see* Pseudofolliculitis barber

Razors, 55

RDA, Recommended Dietary Allowance, 207, 209, 210, 211, 212, 214, 215, 216

Reactions, chemical, 162

Reactions, secondary, 3

Reflexology, an energy-based system of therapeutic massage that manipulates areas on the hands and the soles of the feet to achieve balance in the inner organs, 92

Regeneration, 10

Relaxation tapes, 76

Relaxed hair, *see* Hair relaxation

Reliability of skin care products, 177

Repigmentation, 48

Respiration through skin, 27

Reticular layer, thicker and more densely packed with fibers than the papillary layer, 13–14

Reticulin, 13

Retin-A, 46

Retinol, 171

Retinol A, 184

Riboflavin, 207

Rinses, 123

RNA, ribonucleic acid, 104

Root, the part of the hair that is below the surface, 113

Rosacea, 42

Rosemary, decongests surface tissue and helps heal the skin, 189, 191

Vellus hair, baby hair; it is very short, very fine, and colorless, 110

Ventouses, 79, 86

Vibration, a rapid shaking movement of muscle tissue and can be either soothing or stimulating, 96

Virions, virus particles, 104

Viruses are not living organisms and can only exist and reproduce inside living cells, 104

Vitamin A, 207

Vitamin B complex, 62, 207

Vitamin B$_1$, 207

Vitamin B$_2$, 207

Vitamin B$_3$, 207

Vitamin B$_5$, 207

Vitamin B$_6$, 208

Vitamin B$_{12}$, 208, 213

Vitamin B$_{13}$, 208

Vitamin B$_{15}$, 208

Vitamin C, 209, 213

Vitamin D, 28, 209

Vitamin E, 172, 209–210

Vitamin F, 203, 210

Vitamin H, 208

Vitamin K, 210

Vitamin P, 210–211

Vitamin supplements, 218

Vitamin T, 211

Vitamin U, 211

Vitamins, 203, 205–211

Vitamins, list of, 205–206

Vitiligo, a skin disorder that appears as white patches that come together to erase the coloration in both small and large areas of the skin, 47–50

Volatile organic compounds (VOCs), 164

W

Waste products, elimination of, 8, 22, 27, 93, 200, 201

Water: chemical structure of, 158; in cleansers, 175; in human body, 27, 197; importance of, 216–217; as product extender, 173; sea water, 196–197; and skin care, 164–165; as solvent, 174

Weight, maintaining ideal, 218

Wheat germ masks, 102

White birch, *see* Birch

Whiteheads, 59

Wild Oregon grape, can be effective with a number of skin conditions, including acne, eczema, and psoriasis, 189, 191

Witch hazel, is astringent and antiseptic and has healing properties, 189, 191

Wood's lamp, a black (ultraviolet [UV]) light device, usually coupled with a magnifying lens, 29, 31, 72, 73, 85: and hyperpigmentation, 45

Working environment, safe, 107

Wrinkles: causes of, 38; and mature skin, 33; relieving, 98, 99, 100, 181; smoking and, 41

Y

Yarrow, is astringent and drying and stimulates the circulation, 171, 189, 191

Ylang-ylang oil, is antiseptic and soothing to the skin, 194, 195

Youthful appearance of black skin, 4

Z

Zinc, 213, 216

Zinc oxide, 153, 171